The
Answer
Book

Real Answers for Real Problems
for Parents with Children 3 to 12

Kathleen Yapp

BARBOUR
PUBLISHING, INC.
Uhrichsville, Ohio

The
Answer
Book

© MCMXCVIII by Kathleen Yapp.

ISBN 1-57748-221-2

Scripture quotations are taken from the New King James Version. Copyright© 1979, 1980, 1982 by Thomas Nelson, Inc. Used by permission. All rights reserved.

Published by Barbour Publishing, Inc.
　　　　　　　 P.O. Box 719
　　　　　　　 Uhrichsville, Ohio 44683
　　　　　　　 http://www.barbourbooks.com

ecpa Member of the
      Evangelical Christian
      Publishers Association

Printed in the United States of America.

Acknowledgments

To the dozens of men and women who shared their parental insight with me—*Thanks*, and my prayers are with you.

Dedication

To my children, Lisa, David, Terry, and Jim, who gave me the knowledge and experience to write this book, and my "everything's under control" husband, Ken, who raised them with me and still found time to be my best friend—*Thanks* to all, with hugs and undying love.

Contents

Introduction

I'm sure your children never had a temper tantrum in a supermarket, lived in so messy a room you couldn't enter without danger to life and limb, refused to eat that delectable new seafood dish you fixed for supper, neglected chores, received poor grades in school, sassed you in front of friends, fought against going to church on Sunday, wanted to wear clothes you were sure came from outer space, forgot to say thank you and please, and raised the eyebrows of relatives who now had concrete evidence manners were never taught in your house.

No, I'm sure your children have never caused tension in your home, made you tear your hair out in frustration over trying to understand them and get them to do what you wanted, or made you contemplate running away from home—*but mine have!*

Being a parent is great—it really is. The only problem is that our children have a fantastic knack for twisting us into knots, worrying about whether or not we are "good" parents.

The very fact that you are reading this book shows you are concerned about raising your child to be a responsible, intelligent, genuinely likeable, God-fearing person. Unfortunately, the road to this lofty accomplishment is at times strewn with downright bad behavior, altogether annoying attitudes, and a total inability on the part of the child to appreciate the incredibly bright, loving, responsible parents he or she has been given.

The Answer Book offers just what we parents need: specific answers to specific problems. And these answers come from the real "experts" on child-raising—parents themselves who are now going through, or have encountered in the recent past, every problem and every trial explored in this book.

You won't have to read the entire book to find help. Just turn to the chapter that deals with the problem you are having now. There you'll find a list of down-to-earth, we've-tried-it methods that may contain the solution you've been seeking, one that suits your child's personality and satisfies your own personal standards. Some of these methods you will agree with; others you won't.

Being a parent isn't easy—we all hit times when we just don't know what to do next. When my husband and I were raising our four children, we embraced every bit of knowledge, coupled with common sense, prayer, and faith in the Almighty. Today we're the grandparents of seven precious boys and girls, but times haven't changed. Kids are still kids and now our children are scratching their heads and asking, "What do we do?"

My advice: First, ask God for guidance. Second, ask other parents.

You will survive parenthood.

Kathleen Yapp
(Still alive and kicking. . . .)

CHORES

And whatever you do, do it heartily, as to the Lord and not to men, knowing that from the Lord you will receive the reward of the inheritance; for you serve the Lord Christ.

COLOSSIANS 3:23–24

The egg flew by me, barely missing the bag of groceries I was carrying, and crashed into the refrigerator.

I'd been greeted from a hard day at work by the whooping of my nine-year-old David and his friend, Rusty, and then witnessed the result of their play.

Both boys froze when they saw me, but my attention quickly moved to the shattered egg. Mesmerized, I watched the yolk and the white race each other down the front of the white appliance and fall in slithery plops on the floor.

"Daviiiid!"

Being a bright child, he recognized trouble when he heard it. "Sorry, Mom," he apologized nicely. "I'll clean it up right away."

His friend gave me his most innocent smile.

"Thanks, sweetheart," I said. I put the groceries down on the nearest counter. "You remembered, I hope, that the fire chief from your dad's station and his wife are coming for dinner tonight."

David was already pulling forty sections of paper toweling off the roll from under the sink. "Sure, Mom."

I started unloading lettuce and tomatoes from the bag. "Did you kids do the chores I gave you this morning? I appreciate your help."

"Uh. . .I'm not sure about Terry and Jim and Lisa. What were mine again?"

My hand froze on the lettuce. "You were to take out the garbage. Jim was to sweep the patio. Lisa was to clean her bathroom, and Terry was going to dust the living room."

I walked to the pantry. When I opened the door, a squashed box of Froot Loops toppled off the overflowing trash basket.

"As soon as I finish this," David promised, "I'll do that. Rusty will help."

Why didn't that make me feel better?

I looked out the back door. The patio was strewn with dirty sneakers, a baseball bat and glove, an inside-out motorcycle jersey, the dog's food dish, which had tipped over, and dirt. Murphy, our Irish setter, had been digging in the flower bed again. *Jim, you're in trouble,* I thought.

I turned back and watched for a second as David struggled to clean the shattered egg off the refrigerator door. It looked worse than it had before. Add that to the list of things to do.

"How was school?" I asked him on my way into the living room. I knew I could trust Terry to. . .

"Okay," he answered. "How was work?"

"Hectic." I took in a sudden breath. A delicate layer of dust lay quietly on every piece of furniture in the room, even on the television screen across which my tidy husband had written his name with his finger.

"Where's your brother?"

"Baseball practice," David called out.

Surely the bathroom would be done. I shoved open the door, pushing aside some of my daughter's clothes that lay in a clump on the floor.

"Where's your sister?"

"At Jennifer's."

I returned to the kitchen. "Has that girl been home at all?"

"Nope. She called from Jennifer's."

David carried the soppy paper towel across the kitchen to the trash can, dripping egg yolk and white along the way.

My blood pressure went through the ceiling. I'd just had a nonstop day at the office. Being executive secretary to the president of a national automobile company gave me no time to file my nails. After a forty-five-minute drive on the freeway, I'd made a frantic dash through the grocery store, buying last-minute ingredients for dinner. Now my children, who had promised me faithfully that morning they'd do their chores—"We promise, Mom, we'll do them, don't worry"—had not done their chores and I was beyond worried. I was plotting their house arrest for the next ten years.

I stared at the gooey egg remains on the floor. I thought of the dust in the living room, and Murphy's food on the patio, and the guest bathroom, which was also my twelve-year-old daughter's, and knew I'd never let another human being on planet Earth into that room without scouring it first.

All I had to do was clean the refrigerator, mop the floor, sweep the patio, dust the living room, wash the sink, toilet, tub, and counter in the bathroom, shake out the rug, put up fresh towels, check the Kleenex, clean the mirror, shine the fixtures, and scrape the week-old toothpaste off the shower curtain.

No problem, except that I definitely needed to shower, my hair had to experience a miracle by six-thirty, and if I didn't get that button sewn on my good blue dress, there'd be a gaping hole right in front and Ken would glare at me all evening.

"I'll never trust a kid again as long as I live," I muttered as I grabbed the broom, dust cloth, glass cleaner, paper towels, toilet bowl scrubber, sink and counter spray. . . .

1.

BEGIN CHORES AS EARLY AS POSSIBLE— FROM AGE ONE.

The very first chore Adam had was putting away his toys. I felt that if he were old enough to get the toys out, he was old enough to put them back. I didn't expect them to be in military order. Just put away. Now, at seven, he makes his own bed—a disaster, but made—and takes out the trash every day.

2.

WHEN THEY ARE VERY YOUNG, DO CHORES TOGETHER.

Since our daughter turned three, she follows my wife through the house helping her with the housework. It's a real "together" thing, and they talk while they work. Sometimes after they get a project started, my wife will say to Chelsi, "Could you finish doing this, sweetheart, while I peel the potatoes for dinner?" The answer most often is yes. A direct command to do something has never worked with our daughter, but if it means working together, then she is eager and willing.

3.

PAY FOR CHORES.

I pay my son to do his chores. If he doesn't do them, I withhold his money. "If Mommy doesn't go to work one day," I explain to him, "I won't get paid for that day." Children won't be children forever and they need to learn this real lesson of life.

4.

NO CHORES DONE, NO FAVORITE TV.

Punishment must hurt. If I simply restrict Courtney's TV watching for two days because she has neglected her chores, it won't mean nearly as much as if I restrict her favorite programs.

5.
SUBTLE BRIBERY WORKS GREAT.

If there is something Stephanie wants to do, I'll say, "We'll see when I get home from work. There are some things I must do first." Usually she knows what needs to be done and will have it finished before I get home. At other times when she wants me to drive her somewhere, I'll say, "I have to finish this first." Often she'll suggest, "Let me help." That works better than my griping at her: "Run, run, run. That's all you expect me to do. . .I have other things to take up my time, you know. . . If you'd ever lift a finger to help around this house I'd have more time to take you places. . . ."

6.
DON'T PAY FOR EXTRA THINGS
DONE AROUND THE HOUSE.

For extra chores I just ask. Katie needs to learn there are times when we must work for no pay. I try to instill the idea that it makes us feel good to help other people without always expecting a reward.

7.
GIVE A DEADLINE
IF THE CHILD PROCRASTINATES.

"You have one hour in which to clean your room and dust the furniture. If your chores are not done, we cannot go to the movies."

8.
HAVE HIM DO CHORES
HE CAN SUCCESSFULLY HANDLE.

We used to have Ryan take out the big trash barrels, but they were too heavy for him and he spilled many things. So we changed his chore to emptying the wastebaskets inside and bringing the empty trash barrels in from outside. He does these chores well and takes pride in his accomplishments.

9.
NEVER DEBATE WHETHER OR NOT A CHORE
GETS DONE—IT JUST DOES!

The need to do chores in our home has been established. "We are all part of the family," we tell our children, "and we each have our share to contribute." Our three daughters are expected to keep their rooms clean, clear the table, wash the dishes, and clean their own bathroom. They are, like most kids, not overwhelmed with the desire to have a spotless bathroom, and my wife and I definitely check on them. But they know that no one else will do it for them.

10.
NO ALLOWANCE UNTIL
CHORES ARE DONE.

I'm pretty lenient about when chores get done, but if Tina doesn't have them finished by Saturday afternoon, she gets no allowance. I do my own housework around hers. She's learned not to ask for her allowance until all chores are finished.

11.
TRY A CHART.

We have a chart hanging up in the kitchen showing each day of the week. It's just high enough for four-year-old Janice to reach. Every day there is a chore listed for her to do, and when Janice finishes it, she gets a star or a happy face. On days she doesn't do it, the space is left blank which, fortunately, disappoints her.

12.
A PENNY A POINT.

On the back of the child's bedroom door have a chart made out by days, listing chores that are to be done. Each chore is assigned a number of points depending on the difficulty: make bed, 4 points; empty wastebasket, 1 point; pick up room, 6 points; scrub bathtub after bath, 5 points, and so on.

Whenever a chore is done, mark it on the chart, and at the end of the week, total up the points and give a nickel for each point, or a dime if you want. In the field of business this is called incentive. Be firm and don't give in if the child doesn't make any money. If he tries, on the other hand, he can make as much as he wants.

13.
HOW TO DECIDE FOREVER
WHOSE TURN IT IS.

"I did the dishes yesterday," our son, John, declared to his younger sister, Candy.

"No, you didn't. I did. It's your turn today," she argued.

Because our kids are always bickering about whose turn it is to do a chore, we finally hit on the odd/even system. John was born on 19 October and Candy on 22 November. Whenever they take turns doing anything, we keep track of whose chore it is simply by checking the calendar to see if it's an even or an odd day. This system works perfectly and eliminates *all* quarreling except, that is, when there are thirty-one days in a month. Then usually Dad ends up filling in.

14.
ELIMINATE FINGERPRINTS FOR GOOD.

Have the children be responsible for their own handprints on the wall. This has been a fantastic help in keeping their grimy hands somewhere other than on our nice paneling and woodwork. I've even heard them warning their friends, "Hey, keep your dirty hands off there. I have to wash it." Since we have a two-story house, our son does one floor and our daughter does the other.

15.
LET THEM DECIDE WHICH CHORES THEY WANT.

Once a month the kids get together and take turns choosing what chores they want. We have a general list of nine things, and since there are three children, they each get three. We note on the list whose turn it is to pick first and they pick one chore at a time, not all three at once. Their ages are eleven, nine, and six, and they do the following: empty trash, clear table, do dishes, pick up dog messes in backyard, dust, set table, feed dog, clean fingerprints from walls, and buy milk at the nearby dairy.

16.
MAKE CHORES HABIT-FORMING.

All it takes to get children to do their chores is patience and perseverance, two qualities we parents have in abundance.

17.
REMIND KIDS ONLY ONCE.

Their chores are their responsibility. If they do them, everything will be fine. If they don't, they have a problem with me. I say, "Okay, stop whatever you are doing and go do that chore." That's it. They do it. There's no debating.

18.
IF I HAVE TO TELL HIM
MORE THAN ONCE,
NO ALLOWANCE.

Because Cole is basically lazy, I made the rule that if I have to remind him more than once to do his chores, he won't get his weekly allowance of seventy-five cents. At seven years old he is expected to clean his room, throw away the trash, pick up his clothes, and feed the cat.

When we first started the no chores, no money rule, I had to remind him twice in the first week and I really hated not giving him his money on Saturday. But I knew if I weren't firm, he would forever take advantage. So I gave him nothing. He has been very good about doing his work ever since. All I have to do now is just look in the direction of the neglected chore and he hurries to do it before I say anything.

19.
No Chores,
No Pleasantries.

When the children want something from me and they haven't done their chores, I tell them, "Sorry, I don't feel like it, just like you don't feel like doing your chores."

20.
Monkey See, Monkey Do.

Do your work around the house exactly like the children do their chores. Once, when our four children failed to do their work without being reminded ten times, my husband and I got so disgusted we decided to imitate their behavior. We used the same excuses they used on us a hundred times: "Oh, I'm sorry, I just forgot. . .I'll do it in a minute . . .I just didn't feel like doing it then. . .don't worry, I won't forget."

When the kids came in for dinner they were surprised to see nothing on the table. With a smile I told them, "Oh, I'll do it in a minute," but I never did. They went hungry several nights while their dad and I sneaked out to McDonald's.

I also "forgot" to do the laundry and they were all screaming because they had no clean clothes to wear. Again I cheerfully said, "I'll get it later," but didn't.

I "forgot" to give out allowances, too, and that really hurt. My husband "didn't feel like" fixing the television set. Major catastrophe. One of the boys was bitterly disappointed when his dad "forgot" to pick up a bicycle part he desperately needed.

We were never snide or angry in our comments, just cheerful and pleasant, like the children usually were under the same circumstances. It gave my husband and me great satisfaction to turn the tables, which we did for over a week. The kids learned a major lesson: We depend on each other to do certain things, and when one of us doesn't do his part, it makes it hard on someone else.

CHURCH

And let us consider one another in order to stir up love and good works, not forsaking the assembling of ourselves together, as is the manner of some, but exhorting one another, and so much the more as you see the Day approaching.

HEBREWS 10:24–25

It was an exciting day for my best friend, Pat. Her fourteen-year-old son, Bobby, was going to be baptized at church. Both sets of grandparents were there for the occasion, as well as a favorite aunt and lots of friends.

Her youngest child, three-year-old Brian, was the most excited of all because so many people were fussing over him as well as his big brother. When I arrived Brian rushed up to me on chubby legs and shouted, "Did you know that Bobby is going to be advertised today?"

1.

TEACH YOUR CHILDREN THAT GOING TO CHURCH IS THEIR WAY OF SAYING, "I LOVE YOU, GOD."

We teach our children that we don't only go to church for what *we* get out of it, but for what we can put into it and because it pleases God. "God made us for exactly the same reason we had you," we tell them, "to have someone to love who will love us back and give us pleasure."

I often explain to my son: "God wants us to tell Him we love Him, and the best way to do that is to visit Him regularly in church. You can't love someone and have the relationship be strong and growing if you only talk to Him twice a year, at Christmas and Easter."

2.

GO TOGETHER AS A FAMILY.

Parents should set the precedent that going to church is a family thing. It's not an experience just for young children and women.

3.

DON'T MISTAKE CHURCHGOING FOR FAITH.

Sitting in a pew and singing hymns does not a Christian make. Our Kimberly accepted Jesus as her Savior when she was only five years old because she wanted a personal relationship with God, not because she wanted to be a member of the church, or dress up every Sunday, or see her special friends in class. We carefully teach her that while it is always wonderful to be in church, the real reason we are there is to get to know God better so that He can work in our lives and make them better.

4.
Urge Kids to Go.

Most children won't do a lot of good things unless urged to, and then they find they like them.

5.
Establish at an Early Age Attending Regularly.

The secret is to establish churchgoing when the children are small. When they're very young it's no big deal that you all go together. If they become reluctant along the way, just point out that this is a family endeavor that you feel is vitally important.

Our Becky, who is eleven, doesn't want to go as much anymore, and argues with us that we are "forcing" her to do something she doesn't want. She makes it sound like we are the world's worst parents. We don't get upset with her but point out that because we are conscientious parents, we have to "force" her sometimes to do things she rebels against, like getting shots at the doctor's, having her teeth filled by the dentist, going to school when she wants to stay home. "We do this because we love you and want the best for you," I point out. "A spiritual education is more important to you than a secular one, because the truths you learn at church will last for eternity."

6.
Your Responsibility Is Just to Get Kids There.

You can't make your children believe, but it is your responsibility to expose them to the teachings of God. They may be uninterested in attending church from time to time, but by having them go anyway, you will have a clear conscience that you have them in a place where they will hear better things than they hear on television and in movies. By taking them to church and encouraging their faith, we feel we're giving our three children a foundation they can carry through life, and use when they discover they don't know all the answers after all.

7.
FIND A CHURCH WITH
A POSITIVE ATTITUDE.

When I was a boy my folks took me to a church where all the preacher did was bawl us out every Sunday for how bad we were. I could hardly wait to get out of there each week. I hated it. Then, when I was twelve, we started attending a church where Christianity was presented in a positive, cheerful way. I started learning verses of Scripture that encouraged me and showed me what I could be, with God's help, and that there was a future planned for me by God. What a difference!

We still go to that church, and take our children, and they love to go because they are learning about a God who cares for them and can help them through the trials of every day, rather than the God I knew as a child who, supposedly, only wanted to punish me.

8.
THE CHURCH CAN HELP
YOU RAISE YOUR CHILDREN.

The church has helped in every area in which I've had trouble with my daughter, or might have had trouble. She goes to church three or four times a week, to youth groups, family nights, and twice on Sunday. Even though I don't go myself, I appreciate the tremendous influence the church has on Leslie. She listens to what they say more than to what I say. I understand that because when I was a kid, I'd listen to an outsider more than to my parents, sad to say.

9.
FIND A CHURCH THAT'S GROWING AND ACTIVE.

Scott loves to go to church because he has many friends there and the church does exciting and interesting things, in addition to teaching him serious spiritual lessons. I grew up in a church that was somber and mysterious and I hated going to services because I didn't understand them and they made me feel unhappy and depressed.

10.
CHURCH VERSUS TV.

Don't let your children grow up expecting to be entertained every time they go to church. A church can't always compete with television or movies or baseball games, but we still need the lessons we learn there.

11.
MAKE IT A DISCIPLINE.

There are many temptations to keep me home on Sunday mornings and not at church. But I think it is important to be disciplined about going, just as I am disciplined about showing up at my job every workday. Once, a few years back, I found a good excuse (I thought) not to go to church regularly. It became easier and easier to stay home or do something else. Eventually I backslid. It took me too long to find my way back to the Lord. Disciplined attendance is a valuable lesson I want to teach my son.

12.
LET IT BE A LEARNING EXPERIENCE
FOR THE WHOLE FAMILY.

Since Krista's preschool is run by the same church we attend, she cheerfully attends and enjoys Sunday school. At four years old she enjoys dressing up and taking her pennies for the offering. We encourage her to explain the lesson to us Sunday afternoon and show us any handiwork she has done. She thrives on this attention, while at the same time our questions reinforce what she was taught that morning.

13.
PICK A DYNAMIC CHURCH.

Find a church where there are groups for children that will teach and encourage them along the path you want them to take. If these groups are not dynamic and progressive, youngsters are sure to be bored. Going to church just for the sake of going will not create meaningful experiences for kids.

14.
TAKE THEM WHEN
THEY'RE YOUNG.

My son recently upbraided me for not forcing him to go to church. He is twenty-one. When I was divorced from my first wife she was awarded the children. Then as the years went by, each of my children, one at a time, came to live with me. They had been exposed to church with their mother, but by the time they got to me, wanted no part of it at all. So, I didn't force them. I was so pleased to have the children with me, I didn't want to make it uncomfortable for them.

My oldest son has since told me that was wrong. "Dad, I wish you had made me go," he recently informed me.

I reminded him of when I had taken him, how he'd resisted.

"I know I did," he answered, "but you still should have kept me going."

He is glad we have changed our philosophy with our two youngest children and are taking them with us each Sunday. My older son wants a faith but feels nothing toward God; yet, he won't go himself to find out.

15.
GIVE KIDS A CHOICE OF THE TYPE OF SERVICE TO ATTEND.

At our house there is no question of whether or not the children go to church. They just do, and there is no big to-do about it. We do, however, give them a choice of attending a Sunday school class with youngsters their own age or attending the adult service with us. We enjoy it when they come in with us, but we understand that their class is, no doubt, more meaningful for them. Give them a choice between something and something and not something and nothing.

16.
THINK CAREFULLY BEFORE DECIDING NOT TO GO.

When our children were very young, my husband demanded that I stop going to church or he would divorce me. I did not want to jeopardize my marriage so I made the difficult decision and did as he wanted. I thought I could still worship God myself at home and that I was not giving up my faith by giving up church. My children did not go to church either, and now that they are grown they still do not go.

Today I am divorced from that man and know that I did the wrong thing in letting him force me to give up something I enjoyed so much and which would have been good for the children, too.

17.
SHARE CHURCH
WITH YOUR CHILDREN.

When our ten-year-old started going to church with a friend of his, we thought that was fine. But when he came home and began asking questions that neither my husband nor I could answer, we felt it was time for us to start going. We came to realize that the church, and having a faith, is an essential part of living that should not be neglected.

18.
EXPLAIN WHY YOU
GO TO CHURCH.

Our Sally is a social child who loves to go to church. But we teach her that church is far more than just a place to see her friends. It's the place where we hear the Word of God. "Our pastor prays all week to receive God's Word for us," I explain. "Isn't that exciting? God has a message just for us."

19.
MAKE GOING TO CHURCH
A JOYOUS THING.

We go to church several times a week. It seems that whenever the doors are open, we're there. The children see that we, their parents, enjoy going to church, not from a sense of duty, but because we enjoy worshiping God. We tell four-year-old Richard and five-year-old Jewell that in church we hear the Bible preached and God's Word helps us to live a better life. They know the people there pray for our family, that we will walk in God's will. We tell them about the hope of heaven. They know we like to see our friends there, and they have many friends, too.

I guess we've done all right when we hear them anxiously ask us, "Is it church day? Is it church day?"

20.
CHURCH PEOPLE ARE FAMILY.

One of the main reasons my Becky loves to go to church is that she feels everyone there—young and old—is her family. They care about her, and have cared ever since she was born. She feels these people are going to accept her no matter what. She also knows she's in God's house and she feels close to Him there.

21.
DON'T LIVE AT CHURCH.

Families should be together in church every week because worship, ideally, brings home all those spiritual lessons you've tried to teach the past six days. But don't get carried away with being there all the time. Kids who are forced to attend every family event, sign up for every cherub and handbell choir, and find their own home used for weekly church meetings may pull away from the church eventually.

During the early years of your child's life, being together as a family —at home—is more important than being at every pertinent church function.

CLOTHES

Now if God so clothes the grass of the field. . .will He not much more clothe you, O you of little faith?

MATTHEW 6:30

"Mom," my daughter squealed, dashing into the kitchen just as I put the last of the fudge icing on the devil's food sour cream chocolate chip cake I had made for my husband's birthday, "I need ninety dollars. Quick!"

My spatula slipped and gouged a hole in the side of the cake. I gaped at my firstborn child. "Ninety dollars quick? I don't respond to that kind of demand."

She gave me a gooey kiss. "It's not really a demand, Mom, just an urgent request."

I returned the kiss and asked, "What is this ninety dollars for?"

"A sweater." Sighing, she sank onto a rattan counter stool and eyed the leftover frosting in the mixer bowl.

"What kind of sweater for a twelve-year-old costs ninety dollars?" I inquired.

"It's not the kind of sweater that's important, it's what's on it."

"It better be diamonds for that price."

"Mother! It's got a picture of Chad Davis on it."

"Chad Davis? Who's Chad Davis?"

Lisa stared at me as though I hadn't yet thawed out from the ice age. "Chad Davis, Mother, is only the hottest, the coolest—"

"How can he be the hottest and the coolest?"

Underlining her exasperation, she rolled her pretty blue eyes. "He's the star of the TV show 'California Dreamer.' You know, he's got sun-streaked blond hair and blue eyes that look right through the screen—at me. His mouth tilts up on the sides, and he has a dimple."

"I see."

"You do?"

"Yes, I see, and no, you can't spend ninety dollars for a sweater that has this hot and cool guy with dimples on it."

Lisa groaned and went into a major pout.

"However," I continued, "if you can save seventy-five percent of the money, I'll chip in the rest."

Instant recovery. Big smile. Gangly arms flew around my neck. "Oh, Mom, you're the greatest."

"I guess that's as close to hot and cool as I'll come, right?"

"I love you, Mom."

A month went by. Lisa did everything she could think of to earn money to buy a Chad Davis sweater. I was impressed but surprised when another month slipped by and then a third without a plea to me for my share of the cost for this sweater she could not live without.

Finally, one day I stopped Lisa on her way to school. "How's the money growing for that Chad Davis sweater?"

"Oh, I have it," she replied casually.

"You do? I'm proud of you for working so hard, but why haven't you asked me for what I promised?"

Lisa gasped. "Spend ninety dollars for a sweater with that jerk's picture on it? Mom, where's your brain? Chad Davis is yesterday's news."

1.
MEET HIM HALFWAY.

We finally found a truce in the battle as to which type of clothes Tyler would wear. When he's with his friends, he wears what he wants, even though I groan, but when he's with my friends, he dresses appropriately to my taste.

2.
GIVE GUIDANCE.

I try to guide Hannah as to the proper dress for different occasions. Her school has a strict dress code and sometimes she wants to wear something that causes me to say, "I really don't think that outfit is appropriate for school, do you? But it's fine for at home."

Most of the time she'll go along with me but she still likes to say, "All the other kids wear it." That makes it hard for me to say no. I don't want my daughter to be different from her friends but I do want her to wear clothes that are becoming and proper. My husband is stricter than I am and we sometimes disagree, but Hannah knows how he feels, and I appreciate his not leaving this responsibility totally with me.

3.
LET HIM BUY HIS OWN CLOTHES.

As soon as we felt Dylan was old enough, we let him buy or select his own clothes. Right away he seemed to take better care of them. This did not work, though, with our daughter, who is incredibly sloppy and careless about her clothes.

4.
The Church Can Be Helpful in Teaching Clothes Decorum.

At church my twelve-year-old Katy has been advised not to wear immodest clothes that are tempting to the opposite sex, like bare midriffs, and not to dress immodestly, like going braless. Most of this advice I go along with, and since she believes the church is right, it helps her, and me.

5.
Start Teaching Kids Early About Good Grooming.

Our daughter goes to preschool three times a week and has her own closet and chest of drawers in which her clothes are arranged neatly. My wife helps her coordinate the colors to know what things look good on her and what goes together. Gradually, our daughter is making more and more decisions on her own.

6.
Ignore Clothes on the Floor.

We just close the door to Brendon's bedroom and let the clothes pile up. When everything is out of the closet and thrown here and there, with most of it dirty, he collects all the clothes and deposits them by the washing machine.

7.
LET KIDS DECIDE WHEN THEIR CLOTHES NEED WASHING.

I never pick up Toni's clothes from the floor in her room because I don't know what is dirty and what has just been dumped there. If she wants her clothes washed, she puts them in the hamper. Then I wash them.

8.
NEVER WEAR OTHER PEOPLE'S CLOTHES.

In our family of four daughters we have the rule, "No one is to wear her sister's clothes at any time, under any circumstances. You are not to wear your friend's clothes nor is she to wear yours." I know it's nice to share, but with four girls using the same clothes, there are always things which are dirty, or torn, or being worn by someone else. The bickering is endless and I get worn out trying to arbitrate. Hence the rule.

9.
TAKE THEM SHOPPING AND MAKE IT FUN.

My wife takes our two children shopping with her when she buys their clothes and teaches them not only about color and style but prices. They know they cannot just buy whatever they want, whenever they want.

10.
SET GROUND RULES AHEAD OF TIME WHEN YOU BUY CLOTHES.

When I take my boys shopping, I tell them what we're going to buy ahead of time: "Today we're going to get two pairs of jeans, three shirts, some underwear, and one pair of tennis shoes for each of you." That way they aren't nagging me for a dozen different things. I explain that I only have so much money, and the things I listed are what they need and what will be bought today. They can make a list of the other things they want, and we might get them next time.

11.
DON'T BE A VICTIM.

Kids will put you through the wringer with that old cliche, "Everybody's wearing this." If you don't think certain clothing is proper or becoming to your child, or if the item costs too much, then stick to your guns and say no.

12.
OBSERVE WHAT KIDS ARE WEARING NOWADAYS.

You don't want to embarrass your children by having them wear things way out of date or style. I don't mean you have to submit to fashion trends that are ridiculous and usually outrageously expensive, but by keeping a sharp eye on what's in and what's not, and balancing that with what you can live with as a parent, your children will appreciate your effort.

My wife is more particular than many parents and wants our girls to look like girls. She likes them in dresses, but today, girls don't wear dresses to school. Both Cindy and LuAnn have gone through phases where they've refused to wear a dress at all, even to church. Sometimes I agree with my wife, and sometimes with the girls. I tell my wife, "If you force the kids to dress as youngsters did twenty years ago, they aren't going to fit in. You'll make oddballs out of them." I tell the kids, "There are times to be more feminine than others. Dresses do have a place and grubbies do, too." Somehow we're all still living in the same house!

13.

OBSERVE WHAT YOUR CHILDREN ARE WEARING.

My wife and I both work and are usually in a rush every morning just getting ourselves ready. It was a wonderful day when our two children reached an age when they could not only dress themselves but pick out their clothes as well. What a help! But we both still keep an eye on what they're wearing, and we let them know that. If we must make suggestions, we do it in as loving a manner as possible, without leaving the impression that the child is dumb or color-blind for having chosen a particular outfit.

14.

SET UP AN "EVERY OTHER SATURDAY HAMPER."

If dirty clothes are left on the floor or anywhere but in the dirty clothes hamper, I gather them up and put them in a special "every other Saturday hamper" (EOSH). When Colleen is looking for a particular piece of clothing she can't find, I tell her to look in the EOSH. She knows that if she finds it there, she won't get it back until that Saturday. Clothes have stopped being tossed hither and yon.

15.
TEACH THEM TO WASH
THEIR OWN CLOTHES.

From the time my daughter was ten she's been washing her own clothes. I make it into a game and encourage her ability to separate the colors from the whites and learn the different water temperatures and fabrics. Kimmy is proud of her knowledge and feels good about herself for helping me out. I reward her every once in a while with lunch out, for just us girls.

16.
DON'T GIVE UP.

Tracy loves to wear jeans and hates dresses. I have to put up quite a fight even to get her into a skirt. My little niece, on the other hand, loves wearing dresses, and when Tracy began to notice how many compliments Jenny received, she decided maybe dresses weren't too bad. (This also works with husbands who don't want to wear suits.)

17.
MORE IS NOT
NECESSARILY BETTER.

We never indulge our daughters with a closetful of clothes. They expect hand-me-downs. But we've taught them that, by buying the best, having a few good clothes is better than many changes of inferior garments.

18.
LET KIDS PICK OUT THEIR OWN CLOTHES.

My son, who is ten, and daughter, only four, go with me to buy clothes for themselves. If I just go by myself and bring things home, there are always reasons they don't want to wear them. However, I never let them wander through a department and say, "You pick out what you want," because inevitably they get confused, don't want anything, and won't try anything on. I spot what I want for them and then give them a choice: Would you rather have a striped shirt or a solid shirt? Such an approach does work.

19.
EXPLAIN HONESTLY WHY YOU CAN'T AFFORD TO BUY THEM BRAND-NAME CLOTHES.

Because we home-school our kids, they don't feel the same pressure as other children to wear brand-name clothes and sneakers, but they have asked for them. Consequently, we've taken the time to explain that our budget does not allow spending so much on just a few pieces of clothing. We show them how much money we have for clothes over the next few months and have them help us allot various amounts for slacks, shirts, dresses, underwear, shoes, and so on. They respond because we respect their judgment and are less demanding.

20.

GIVE CHILDREN THE MONEY FOR THEIR CLOTHES AND LET THEM SHOP ON THEIR OWN.

When our ten-year-old Casey continually berated me for not buying her more clothes, despite the fact that I had patiently explained my budget and had given her the standard line that money doesn't grow on trees, I finally decided to let her see for herself how hard it is to stretch a dollar. I gave her the entire amount I planned to spend on clothes, in cash. Although I went with her to the shopping center so I would be there to advise her, she was basically on her own.

"You may buy whatever you want," I said, thinking as I heard my own voice that it was a crazy woman talking. "But remember that the money you have in your hot little hands is all there is for your clothes this fall."

I could not believe how beautifully this worked. Casey came back to me again and again, appalled and dismayed at how little her money would buy.

Then I gave her lesson two: We went to some discount stores where she found things she liked for a fraction of the cost at retail stores. She felt very grown-up because I respected her ability to see the reality of the world of money, and I felt good because she respected my judgment.

21.

IF THEY WANT BRAND-NAMES, LET THEM HAVE BRAND-NAMES (IF THEY GET THEM WITH THEIR OWN MONEY).

I cannot afford to buy brand-name clothes but I allow my children to buy them IF they can afford to with *their own* money. If Jenna is willing to work hard and long hours to buy a particular kind of jeans, then more power to her. We adults aren't that different when we want a certain kind of car or to live in a certain neighborhood in a certain kind of house. We work harder to achieve our dreams. I see nothing wrong with kids learning to do the same.

22.
Looking Great Is More Important Than Wearing Certain Labels.

I've trained my children to want to look cute or sophisticated instead of depending on labels to make them feel well dressed. "Just because clothes cost a lot does not mean they look good on you," I tell them. I teach them about fabrics and colors and style for various ages.

23.
For Christmas/Birthday I Buy Them One Label.

For the kids' birthdays and for Christmas, I buy them at least one piece of clothing that has a brand name that "all the kids" are wearing now. *But* I buy such items at outlet stores and get them for half the price I'd have to pay in a retail store. I've taught Kristen and Cody not to expect an entire wardrobe of brand names, but if they have at least a few things, they don't feel out of it with their peers.

24.
Stay in Charge of Your Children's Clothes.

It's all the rage in our town to wear baggy pants. Unfortunately, this kind of outfit is what gang members wear. Kids feel "cool" when they dress like that, even if they're not in a gang. Because I have refused to get my boys these pants, my sister told me, "Since you're not going to get them these pants, I will for Christmas."

"Then they'll go right back to the store," I said. "I don't want my kids emulating gang members. Please honor my wishes."

She did, and I've talked the boys out of wanting them too by explaining why gangs are bad.

25.
"WHAT WOULD JESUS DO?"
BRACELETS ARE IN STYLE AND WORTHWHILE.

Kids love wearing WWJD bracelets, the initials standing for "What would Jesus do?" They come in different fabrics, colors, and sizes. When kids are tempted to do something wrong or questionable, they can look down at this bracelet and ask themselves what Jesus would do in their situation. These bracelets only cost about a dollar and are available at most Christian bookstores.

DEATH

And God will wipe away every tear from their eyes; there shall be no more death, nor sorrow, nor crying. There shall be no more pain, for the former things have passed away.

REVELATION 21:4

When one of my son's friends died in a tragic accident, our whole family grieved. Later we talked about what had happened. With a winsome smile on his face, David said, "Mom, if I die before you, I don't want you to be sad. You know I'll be in heaven, with Jesus, and Grandma and Grandpa Peterson. I've had a great life. We've had good times together."

He was the parent; I, the child.

1.

LET HIM EXPERIENCE THE CIRCUMSTANCES OF DEATH.

A child should not grow up with the unrealistic concept that people live forever, or that death will never touch him or his family.

2.

TALK ABOUT IT WITH HER.

"Mommy, when I die, will you go with me?"

"No, dear, dying is something you do alone."

If this frightens her, remind her that she was born by herself and she made it all right and you were there afterward to take care of her. "Even though Mommy can't die with you, Jesus will be there in heaven to greet you."

3.

TELL YOUR CHILD THE TRUTH: NOT EVERYONE WHO DIES GOES TO HEAVEN.

Being a Christian, I know this to be true, but it's a hard concept to teach a child too young to grasp its significance. When my son was nine, and gave his heart to Jesus, I explained how such a decision would affect his death. I really get upset with all the sentimentality in the movies and on television where people with no heart for God die and a child is told, "Mommy went to heaven," or even worse, "Mommy's now an angel." It just isn't true, and a child needs to learn who will and will not go to heaven as soon as he is old enough to understand.

4.
TELL HIM THE TRUTH ABOUT DEATH.

My son, who is seven, never thought about death. Whenever he did see death depicted, for example, on television, it was the cowboys-and-Indians type of scene. But when the mother of one of his friends was suddenly killed, he was totally shaken. Soon afterward he began showing unusual concern for his father and me. Every single day when I'd go to work, he'd say, "Drive carefully, Mom." He diligently waged a stop-smoking campaign against his dad.

One night I found him crying in his room. We talked about death and he admitted that he was scared that his father and I were going to die and leave him. I told him the truth. "I can't tell you that I'll never die because that's not true. We're all going to die. But there is a better place to go if we've loved the Lord and tried to do what He wants. Someday we'll all be together again in heaven. I hope to live until I'm very old and you have children, but it's something I can't worry about because I just don't know what's going to happen in my life."

He was remarkably mature during that talk and I believe came to understand the mystery of death a little better.

5.
INSTILL IN YOUR CHILDREN A KNOWLEDGE
THAT THEY CAN SURVIVE.

I want my children to be strong so they can survive without me, if necessary. In all my training, I've strived to help them learn to do things for themselves. Whenever we talk of death, I emphasize that this is a time when we must be especially strong and take care of those around us who may be grieving. Sometimes I joke with my daughter and say, "Well, if anything ever happens to me, I'm at peace knowing that you can take care of your father and three brothers and run this house by yourself." Even though the thought is not pleasant, still she knows she could do the job and survive on her own.

6.
DON'T EXPOSE KIDS TOO EARLY TO DEATH.

When his father died, my husband insisted on taking our seven-year-old to the funeral. When Ethan saw his grandfather lying in the casket, a much-loved figure in his life, he became hysterical. We had to take Ethan from the room and both of us missed the funeral while we tried to calm him down and explain why his grandpa wouldn't be able to play with him anymore. I don't think I would take a child to a funeral until he's at least twelve years old.

7.
DON'T KEEP YOUR OLDER CHILDREN AWAY FROM SOMEONE WHO'S DYING.

My twin boys were twelve when their mother died of cancer. In the hospital, as Mary slipped away, the entire family was there: her mother and father, brothers and sisters, and me. I did not let my boys go, though, thinking the situation was too traumatic.

Not long ago I found that was a mistake, at least for one of them. My sons are now grown men and I learned that Robert has never forgiven me for being excluded from that scene. Raymond understands that I wanted them to remember their mother as she was when she was vibrantly alive, but Robert finally told me he's resented my doing that all these years. I never knew.

8.
ANSWER YOUR CHILD'S QUESTIONS ABOUT DEATH.

Here's a good piece of advice I was given once: Explain to your child only what he particularly wants to know. Don't go into a complicated, detailed account of death until he's ready for such an explanation. My eight-year-old daughter was crushed when a little friend of hers was run over by a car and killed. As I comforted her, Susan asked me about death, and I answered each question as best I could, but went no further than her inquiries.

9.
WAIT UNTIL THEY'RE INTERESTED TO DISCUSS DEATH.

Until a child wants to know about death, I don't advise even bringing up the subject. If there is a current situation in the child's life that has a bearing on death, such as when an animal dies, or a friend or relative, then let the child ask the questions and you as the parent give the answers.

10.
DON'T PROJECT YOUR FEARS ONTO CHILDREN.

Six months ago my nephew died. He was ten. His three-year-old sister was remarkably calm and full of questions that her parents, who were consumed with vindictiveness against the doctors and hospital, answered with impatience, hysteria, and anger. I watched this happen with great sadness because all kinds of fears were projected onto this young child who could have been helped to understand death and cope with it. Now she thinks death is a nightmare that a family never gets over.

11.
HELP THE CHILD SAY GOODBYE.

When my father was dying at home, my nine-year-old son spent a lot of time talking with him. He knew his grandpa would not be with us much longer, and he was gratified that the two of them could say things that needed saying. My father had not been very good at saying "I love you" to his family but he said it then. To this day my son has happy memories of those talks with his grandpa.

12.
LET THE CHILD
SEE THE BODY.

When my sister died, my little boy wanted to see the body. Since he was only seven I wasn't sure this was a good idea. I said, "You should remember Aunt Helen the way she was when she was alive."

"I will," he answered matter-of-factly, "but I want to see what she is like dead."

I just happened, at that time, to read an article about how important it is for people to see the body of a deceased person. Without that experience there is always the feeling that death did not really occur, and one can live with that unreality for many years.

As I watched my son's face as he peered into the casket, I noticed he did not cry but seemed filled with curiosity as he gazed at her. Then he shocked me. "All right, Mommy," he said turning from the casket, "we can go on with our lives now. Aunt Helen is really dead."

13.
LET YOUR CHILD
SHOW HIS GRIEF.

Don't try to keep a child from crying over a lost loved one, even if that crying is hard and long. He is dealing with his grief and needs to work through that sorrow. Some hospitals have what they call "screaming rooms" where the grieving family can go to scream, cry, pound the wall, pace, call relatives, sit and ponder, and pray. It's okay to grieve.

14.
EXPLAIN THE DIFFERENCE BETWEEN ANIMALS DYING AND PEOPLE DYING.

Our son, Jason, was devastated when our dog died, and he kept asking over and over again if Caesar were going to be in heaven. This was a good opportunity for us to explain the difference between people dying and animals dying. We told Jason that Caesar might very well be in heaven because God loves us and heaven will be filled with everything wonderful that we like. However, because Caesar does not have a soul, he will not be judged like human beings. This helped Jason understand the concept of getting his heart right with the Lord, and the necessity of doing that.

15.
SINCE WE ARE CHRISTIANS, WE CAN ASSURE OUR CHILDREN THAT WE'RE ALL GOING TO BE TOGETHER AFTER DEATH.

When Scott's favorite uncle died, this prompted our son to ask where we were all going to be after we died. Although we had already talked about heaven, this gave us another opportunity to explain that, as Christians, we knew we would go to live with Jesus, and we would know each other there.

16.
WE TALK FREELY ABOUT HEAVEN AND WHAT WE THINK IT'S LIKE.

Whenever someone we know dies, we talk about it freely, bringing up the idea that if they loved Jesus they will go to heaven, their new life, where they'll wear a crown. The children like to visualize people wearing crowns with jewels and walking on streets paved with gold.

17.
BE PATIENT WHEN CHILDREN STRUGGLE TO ACCEPT DEATH.

Our eight-year-old, Nicholas, had a desk partner in school who was killed in a house fire. He grieved for her but didn't know it. The rest of the family knew his feelings, though, because for the longest time he was angry and denied that the girl had even died. "She just moved away and doesn't want to come back," he insisted.

Then he really got hung up on everybody dying. "Daddy's going to die at work today. . .you're going to die driving in the fog. . .Grandma's going to die because she's flying here on a plane. . .I'm going to die. . . ."

We explained to him that it was unusual for a child to die, that neither his father nor I died as children, and that he, Nicholas, probably wouldn't either. I wasn't certain whether to insist that he accept that the girl from school had died rather than moved away, but since she was not a member of our family I didn't push the fact.

He dropped the subject for a few months, then he came home from school one day and said, "Mom, Ingrid is extinct."

"What?" I said. A unit on dinosaurs had finally made his classmate's death a reality.

18.
LET THE VETERINARIAN EXPLAIN TO YOUR CHILD WHY HER PET SHOULD BE PUT TO SLEEP.

When we had to have our dog put to sleep, our daughter overreacted. "You're killing Bobo," she cried at us. "He doesn't want to die." The day we did "the deed," I had to pick Kimmy up at school because she was so upset. Then I decided to take her to the veterinarian and let him tell her why Bobo had needed to be put out of his misery. Kimmy listened with eyes wide open to the simple explanation. She cried a little and then wanted to see the room and the table where it had been done. Because a professional had explained the matter to her, she knew it wasn't just a whim on our part that had made us take away her beloved pet. She never blamed us again for doing something wrong.

19.
IF YOUR CHILD IS GOING TO DIE, TELL HIM.

While James was growing up, he had fears that are common to most children: the dark, being left alone, loud noises. In each case, we could ease his fear if we explained to him what was happening or why. Fear of the unknown is something we all face but knowledge makes coping possible.

When James went into the hospital with leukemia at the age of nine, he was terrified at all that the doctors and nurses were doing to him. We asked the doctors to explain to James exactly what each procedure was, when he was tested or had therapy, and this helped him go on.

When we knew he would not live much longer, we agonized for many days wondering whether or not to tell him. Finally, we decided it would relieve his fear if he knew the truth, because he surely suspected something terrible.

Again we asked a kind doctor to explain to James what was happening inside his body. Then my husband and I and our family took over. Since James had always gone to church, and had given his heart to Jesus when he was seven, he understood that there was a place called heaven, and now we could prepare him for his next journey. I can't say it was easy, or that it didn't break our hearts, but James accepted the inevitable with more courage than I had expected, and I am sure it is because he knew the truth. Jesus said, "You shall know the truth, and the truth shall make you free."

20.
IT'S JUST A SIMPLE MOVE FROM
ONE PLACE TO ANOTHER.

A minister came to our church recently and related this story. His four-year-old son had asked him, "Daddy, what is death like?" His answer: "Do you remember last night when you were so tired you just fell asleep out here in the living room?"

His son nodded yes.

"Then I came along and picked you up in my strong arms and carried you into your own bedroom where you woke up this morning?"

Again the boy agreed.

"Death is like that. We fall asleep in one room, and God picks us up in His strong arms and carries us to our own room in heaven. When we wake up, everything is fine and wonderful and we can talk to Jesus."

Divorce

Therefore a man shall leave his father and mother and be joined to his wife, and they shall become one flesh.

GENESIS 2:24

My next-door neighbor, Betty Belle, can find humor in just about every situation. One night her husband, Michael, came home from work in a rotten mood.

"I noticed it right away," she told me. "He yelled at the canary to stop singing when it wasn't making a peep, and then he threw the paper at the couch instead of onto it. Angela [their-six-year-old] noticed, too.

"'Uh-oh,' she said, 'Daddy wants a divorce.'

"My mouth dropped open," Betty Belle said, "and so did Michael's. 'He does?' 'I do?' we said at the same time.

"'Oh, yes,' Angela assured us. 'My friend, Sissy, at school, said her daddy got mad one day and then got a divorce.'

"She was so serious, and concerned, that Michael broke down and laughed. I did, too," Betty Belle admitted. "What a way to get out of a bad mood, was all I could think, but wasn't about to say—not with a divorce looming over my head."

1.

Don't Accept Divorce as an Easy Way Out.

Several of our children's friends have parents who are divorced. We never criticize a couple who's ended their marriage but rather use the situation to talk with our kids when they wonder why it happened. We ask questions like, how did the couple get to that place? What could they have done to keep their marriage together? We are amazed at how clearly children can assess problems. Their solutions are often as good as ours.

2.

Model Commitment Before Your Kids.

If your children are taught early that marriage means commitment, then even when they see you disagree with your spouse, they will know you are determined to find ways to solve problems other than by divorce or separation. No family should live with the fear that you will break up. In fact, modeling commitment can apply to many facets of life.

"Anyone can quit a marriage, a job, a friendship," my husband tells our two sons, "but sticking to it requires something more, and that something is commitment."

It isn't always easy to stay committed, but it's a principle we believe in, and model.

3.

Answer Their Questions the Best You Can.

Be prepared to answer the Big Question: How can people get divorced when they were both so happy to get married? When I got divorced, I explained to my daughter, "Yes, your daddy and I were happy in the beginning but sometimes the years change people. Daddy started to hit me when he got angry and that is very wrong."

Since Brianna had seen several such scenes, and had been terrified during them, she understood why I couldn't stay married to her daddy. "We'll still love him," I told her, "and pray for him." We had just started going to church, Brianna and I, and had been learning of the power of prayer.

"Can we pray that Jesus will teach Daddy how to love and not hit?" she asked.

"Yes, we certainly can." And we did. And one day, her daddy came back to us.

4.
TRY NOT TO DAMAGE YOUR CHILD'S FAITH IF YOU GET DIVORCED.

Our children know that our faith and our church do not take divorce lightly. They know their daddy has a girlfriend and he didn't deny it when our eleven-year-old son saw him with her. Our youngest son, at four, doesn't understand why that woman can't come and live with us. Why does his daddy live somewhere else?

It is particularly difficult for me to explain the pending divorce without sounding like I'm trying to get them to side with me against their father. Since we had taught them, during normal family squabbles, the importance of talking together to work things out, they understand how deep the problem is between their daddy and me when I tell them he won't talk with me about it, or go to a minister or Christian counselor for help.

5.
DON'T EXPOSE THEM TO YOUR EMOTIONS.

We didn't let our children hear the bitter arguing. Their dad left the house several months before we moved and still sees the children frequently. They know their dad loves them and their mom loves them, but their parents don't get along together.

6.
Don't Assume Your Children Are Too Young to Understand.

I handled it all wrong. When my wife and I got divorced, my philosophy was, okay, Jan and I are splitting up, this is our problem. The boys are too young to understand. I gave Jan the burden to explain or not explain about the divorce.

The boys at first would ask me, "How come you don't live here anymore?"

I wouldn't give them an answer. I figured they were with their mother ninety percent of the time and I didn't want to give them a different answer from what she was saying. I trusted her to say the fair thing but she didn't, and now I wish I could explain my side but the kids aren't interested anymore. If I had it to do again, I would be more sympathetic to the children's needs, and not so concerned about mine.

7.
Tell Your Children the Truth.

When my husband began to abuse me, I excused it for a while but then decided I could not live in that environment, and I did not want my children raised in such a home. It's been hard to explain that to them because I don't want to make their father look bad in their eyes. But both Kevin and Kerry have seen Neil strike me, and it frightened them, so they're taking it better than I supposed. I know some people think I should stick it out, no matter what, but until you live with the fear of being beaten every day, you cannot know the horror of such a marriage.

8.
DON'T COP OUT WHEN THE GOING GETS ROUGH.

When things are tough, don't say to the child, "Go call your father. Ask him." I did that for the first six months after my divorce and it really hurt my child because she got the impression that if she couldn't get everything she wanted from me, she could hit up good old Dad. Her father was put in a bad spot not knowing whether something was good for her or not.

9.
BE CAREFUL WHAT YOU THREATEN.

My daughter went though a rebellious stage when she would not do anything I wanted. She didn't like any of the rules of the house and conduct that applied to her. Finally one day, in desperation, I said, "Maybe you'd like to go live with your father."

To my dismay, her eyes lit up and she said, "Yes, I would."

Confident that my former husband would support me in how I was trying to raise Amber, I called him and let him talk with her after I had first explained what was happening. I was wrong. He told Amber she could live with him if she wanted.

I was devastated, not only at the thought of losing my daughter, but because I didn't want her raised in an environment where a twelve-year-old makes the rules instead of an adult.

Amber lived with her father for one year then begged to come back home. She missed me, her brothers, all her friends, and her school, she told me. She was lonely. "There will still be rules to follow," I reminded her before agreeing she could return, but she anxiously accepted these and has been wonderfully cooperative since.

10.
ACT YOURSELF.

Kyle was two when Bob and I divorced and I thought that at that age he wouldn't notice much. But he had been extremely close to his father and I was amazed at the change in him. He wouldn't eat or sleep. At night he ground his teeth for hours. And he cried and cried. I didn't know what to do. I felt so guilty, as though the divorce had all been my fault.

So I tried to placate him. I pampered him, paid more attention to him. I went too far trying to make up to him for the loss of his daddy.

Finally, his pediatrician told me I should just act like a normal mom. The pampering and smothering had made him feel more insecure because he knew that was not the real me, the one he was used to. So I tried to be the mother he had had before the divorce, and although it wasn't easy, it helped me to get over the pain, too. After about a year and a half, my son had adjusted to the change in our lives, and so had I.

11.
DON'T BE AFRAID TO ARGUE
IN FRONT OF YOUR CHILDREN.

Our number-one mistake was that we never fought in front of our children. We kept our disagreements for private times. Unfortunately, when we separated, it hit the kids with unbelievable force. One day we were together and seemingly happy with each other, and the next day Daddy was gone and Mama was crying all the time.

If I could do it again, I would allow the children to see disagreements occasionally—not all the quarrels, of course, but enough for them to understand what their parents' marriage was really like.

When I try to explain to them about the divorce and tell them that their father and I just can't get along and that we fight when we're together, they become hostile toward me because they think I'm lying. They haven't seen any of that. They've only seen harmony.

12.
BE PATIENT
WITH THEIR THREATS.

When he thought I was being particularly mean to him, Johnny told me he wanted to go live with his daddy. The first time he said it, I sloughed it off. When he said it again a couple of weeks later, I had a talk with him and explained that as long as he was under eighteen, he would have to live with me. I thought that would stop the threats but I was wrong.

Finally, when he said it once too often, I decided to call his bluff. "Okay," I said, "if that's what you really want, I'll call your daddy and he can come and get you." Johnny was four-and-a-half at the time.

For about two hours he was totally happy, until I started to pack his things. "Who can I give this bed to?" I asked him.

His face fell. "Why are you giving my bed away?"

"You won't be here anymore," I answered.

"But I'll come and see you."

"Yes," I agreed, "but you won't need this bed. Let's see, these toys can be given away, and you won't have a use for this little collar for Toby [our cat]."

Johnny's mouth fell open and I thought he was going to cry. "Isn't Toby going with me?" he sobbed.

"No, dear, Toby's my cat, so he must stay here. Now what do you want to take with you?" In just a few minutes Johnny decided that he liked where he was. He never asked to live with his dad again.

13.
DON'T SAY ANYTHING NEGATIVE ABOUT
YOUR FORMER SPOUSE, IF POSSIBLE.

This is really a hard one, but if at all possible, try not to cut down your child's father or mother. The disagreements are between you parents and not the children. You will only make your child resent you and your comments and cling protectively to the maligned parent. Children are staunch defenders of an absent parent. At least mine were.

14.
DON'T EXPLAIN A DIVORCE THROUGH YOUR EYES ALONE.

Children have a tough time understanding lines like, "Mommy is happier without Daddy. . .we can still live a good life without him. . .he made me unhappy." They only see that they are now missing a father, and they don't say to themselves, "Now Mom will be happy 'cause Dad's gone." They will still feel the absence and somehow you'll have to compensate for that void.

Expect them to have thoughts on how the other parent feels, and try not to be hurt by their comments. At the same time, don't be afraid to defend yourself: You can only defend the other parent just so much before your own authority will be jeopardized.

15.
AT ALL TIMES BE HONEST WITH YOUR CHILDREN.

When Jack and I were first divorced, he took our daughters every weekend. Then it got to be every other weekend, then once a month. Then every few months. The children were devastated. They couldn't understand why their father didn't want to see them. Although I was tempted to run him down, I tried honestly to answer why he wasn't seeing them. "Your dad would like to see you, I'm sure, but he is very, very busy," I would say, or, "Your father wants to wait until he has a nicer place for you to stay," and this was true, for their father hated his new apartment and was acutely embarrassed to bring his children there.

16.
LET YOUR CHILDREN CONTINUE
TO LOVE THEIR OTHER PARENT.

Such a strategy is nigh on to impossible in some circumstances, but it's far better to let the children form their own opinions about their absent parent. If you try to force your judgment down their throats, they will rebel, even if they know they're wrong. Let them talk about their father or mother all they want. Agree. Nod your head. Even throw in a few nice comments now and then.

17.
ASSURE YOUR CHILDREN THAT
YOU WILL NOT GET A DIVORCE.

Corben's best friend's parents got a divorce and this upset our son. He became moody and unresponsive around the house. It took us weeks to finally discover that he was afraid we would get a divorce, too. We listened carefully to his anxieties and then comforted him by saying we would never get a divorce because we loved each other and were deeply committed to our marriage. Most importantly, we told Corben, as Christians, we could ask God for wisdom to deal with problems that could lead to divorce.

The bottom line: He needed assurance over and over that we were not going to separate.

18.
PEOPLE WHO GET DIVORCED
ARE NOT WICKED.

Someone told our daughter, who is eleven, that anyone who is divorced is a bad person. Of course, we told her that was not true. "They might be misguided, or confused, or unhappy now," my husband told her, "but that does not mean they are not nice people. Marriage is not always easy. One has to work at it, just as you have to work at sharing a room with your sister."

Serena understood that comparison very well because she loves her sister but does not always like being around her or the things she does.

19.
The Time for Learning Is Before Marriage.

We feel very strongly that commitment and loyalty and a shared Christian faith are the things that hold a marriage together. So it's only natural that we've taught our daughter, who's twelve, how important it is to be sure her partner feels the same way she does before they get married. We stress the importance, after marriage, of working out problems. However, if adultery or physical abuse occurs, and a couple can't work out their differences through Christian counseling, then divorce should be considered, but only as a last resort.

20.
Adultery May Justify Divorce.

Because I was raised in a church that does not sanction divorce, I stayed with my husband for over thirty years, putting up with his blatant infidelities, lack of support, and indifference (we did not sleep together the last ten years). We raised four children in that hostile atmosphere, and I know our marriage was a terrible example for them. Only one of our children is happily married today; the other three don't want anything to do with marriage.

I started going to a dynamic evangelical church with a friend of mine and, after six months, found the Lord Jesus as my personal Savior. I was surprised to learn the Bible allows divorce in cases of adultery. I wept for all the wasted years I'd stayed in that abusive marriage.

The next time Paul asked me for a divorce, I said yes. It was traumatic for me, and for the children, although by that time they were grown and on their own. Finding a job after I had stayed in the home all those years was difficult, but now I do work I enjoy, have many new friends, a higher self-esteem, money to spend the way I choose (and I choose to travel, which I never did before), and I'm happy. I praise the Lord for that deliverance.

Faith in Action

Train up a child in the way he should go, and when he is old he will not depart from it.

PROVERBS 22:6

When your children grow up and look back on their childhood, what one picture of you will they retain in their minds? What will they see you doing?

I have the picture of my father, who was a minister, studying the Bible at his desk. I see him with several translations of the Scriptures before him, commentaries, paper, and pen, making notes for sermons.

I rarely interrupted those times of study, not because he demanded I not, but because I knew this was his special time to be with and learn about the Lord, and to receive God's message for His people.

Right now, as I write this, I can see in my mind's eye my father, Lawrence Adelbert Peterson, sitting at his mahogany desk, studying his Bible.

1.
ALWAYS EXPLAIN TO A CHILD WHY YOU BELIEVE WHAT YOU DO.

Doctrine is not only for grown-ups. The strongest adult Christians I know are those who had their faith explained to them when they were young. They weren't just told, "You have to believe this because we, your parents, believe this, and Grandmother Smith believed this, and her parents before her did. . . ." There are some wonderful books to be read and discussed with a child, written in very simple terms, that explain about God, Jesus, and the Holy Spirit, sin, heaven, and hell.

2.
LIVE YOUR LIFE BEFORE THEM.

Until last year my wife and I were not Christians. But then an evangelist came to a nearby church, one attended by a neighbor of ours. When Fred invited us to go to one of the meetings, we agreed reluctantly and only out of respect for him. No one was more surprised than we were when we gave our lives to the Lord on the fourth night of the revival.

Since that night life has changed completely for Nancy and me. The children, though, who are eight, eleven, and twelve, aren't thrilled with these changes. They don't want to go with us to church but we're taking them anyway. There's so much for us all to learn. We have Christian literature around the house, pray together every day, and listen to evangelical television and radio broadcasts, but not in excess. Our pastor suggested we simply live our new lives in Christ before our children and let them "see" the differences in us. Hopefully, they'll want the joy we now have.

3.
TAKE TIME TO EXPLAIN CHRISTIAN HOLIDAYS.

I remember telling our three-year-old daughter why we celebrate Christmas instead of Hanukkah (she has a Jewish friend). "That's because we're Christian," I told her.

She squinted her eyes, trying to understand. "Daddy, is Mommy a Christian?"

"Yes," I said.

"And you're a Christian?"

"Yes."

"Is Rufus [our dog]?" I had a little more explaining to do.

4.
TEACH YOUR CHILDREN TO PRAY.

Our daughter attended a Christian school where she learned structured prayers. When she was about six years old, my wife taught her to break out from the memorized prayers and to say what she felt, for indeed she was talking to God. It was very moving to hear her praying as though talking to a special friend: "Thank You for making me well, and thank You for my food today. . . ."

5.
BE SURE A CHILD KNOWS HE MUST
HAVE HIS OWN RELATIONSHIP WITH GOD.

We pray at mealtimes and have a short devotion around the table with our children, but then we excuse them to go to their rooms and have their own time with the Lord. They each have a children's Bible and some well-illustrated Bible storybooks. "You need to develop your own walk with God," we tell them. "Talk to Him. Listen to Him. Let Him lead you."

6.
IT STARTS WITH PRAYER.

We take turns praying at every mealtime. Even our youngest, Susan, who is four, says a prayer for our food.

Then the children always say their prayers at night before they go to bed. I encourage them to come to me with any question they may have about God. The other day Susan asked, "Where did God get His name?"

I thought for a moment, then said, "He named Himself."

She nodded as though fully understanding. "I'm going to name myself, too."

"Oh?"

"Yes," she declared. "I want to be God's Susan."

I hugged her. "What a wonderful name," I said.

7.
FAMILY BIBLE STUDY SHOULD
BE AT THEIR LEVEL OF INTEREST.

Three times a week, on Mondays, Wednesdays, and Fridays, we have a five-minute Bible reading right after dinner. We remove the dishes from the table, then stay there and either Bob or I reads a portion of Scripture.

"Do you have any questions?" we ask our two girls, Jessica and Jayme, who are nine and eleven. Sometimes they do but most often they don't, so we send them off to their rooms so they can read in private again the Scripture from their children's Bibles. "If you have any thoughts about what you read, or any questions, share them with Mommy or me when you finish," we tell them.

They are only asked to spend five minutes or so in their own private devotions. Most of the time, though, they stay with it longer. But the choice is theirs. We want them to enjoy reading God's Word, and it's better if they delve into it themselves than have us dictate a long time of study. The questions they've come up with amaze us—and show us they really are thinking about what they're reading.

8.
THERE'S AN ANSWER IN SCRIPTURE FOR EVERY NEED.

The conference with our son's kindergarten teacher did not go as we'd expected. Walking down the halls of the public elementary school afterward, I glanced sideways at my husband, Brett. He was wiping his face with his red handkerchief, but a single tear fell from his chin. Tears welled in my eyes, too.

Here we were, two well-educated adults, one with a doctorate in chemistry, who had just been told our five-year-old Jeremy would have to repeat kindergarten. Repeat kindergarten? Our bright son?

In the weeks and months that followed, we located an excellent private school that, providentially, had an opening in kindergarten the following fall. We weren't able to afford this ivy-covered education, but we convinced those nearest and dearest of our dire need and they helped us with the tuition.

As Christians, we thought we knew the Bible pretty well, but a sermon given by a former pastor on a summer Sunday before the start of our son's second kindergarten experience changed our minds. The pastor read from the Book of James, chapter 1, verses 5 and 6: "If any of you lacks wisdom, let him ask of God, who gives to all liberally and without reproach, and it will be given to him. But let him ask in faith, with no doubting, for he who doubts is like a wave of the sea driven and tossed by the wind."

Did God really mean I could ask Him to help my son get through kindergarten? Or did God define wisdom as something more befitting Solomon than a six-year-old? Then there was my faith in question: Did I believe God could do what I asked. . .if it were in His will?

On that first day of school for Jeremy, I began praying these verses, fervently, pleadingly, openly. And I have prayed them every year since.

God's answers to my prayers, and those of my husband, were not immediate and not exactly according to our "master" plan. Jeremy "graduated" from kindergarten, then first, second, and third grades, still struggling—but blessed. God's hand was definitely on him, and he now possessed an eagerness to learn and a top-notch feeling of self-worth. We transferred him to a Christian school in fourth grade and began to see God's blessings in overflowing abundance. By the time

The Answer Book

Jeremy graduated from middle school in eighth grade, he had garnered almost every academic award possible.

God does grant wisdom to parents—and to children—who seek answers in His Word to seemingly unfathomable crises.

9.
CHILDREN LIKE HAVING BOTH MOM AND DAD THERE FOR DEVOTIONS.

Both my wife and I take time from our other tasks to be together when we have a structured Bible study with Cassey, our seven-year-old. She loves being with us—and, of course, we love being with her. We use a children's Bible that breaks the main stories into short segments that each take only five minutes to read. The basic outline of the story is given and the main characters are introduced. With Cassey's natural curiosity, these stories are perfect for her. We've been through this book twice and are now on the third read-through.

We also use faith-building videos. One of Cassey's favorites involves puppets that teach biblical conduct and such parenting goals as getting along and problem solving.

We spend about fifteen to twenty minutes on the study. It's the best twenty minutes of the day for my wife and me. What could be better than giving your child a firm understanding of God's love and importance!

10.
MEMORIZED PRAYERS CAN LEAD TO HEARTFELT PRAYERS.

We're helping Brianna to learn to pray. She can recite the "Now I lay me down to sleep. . ." prayer. Then I pray, and about half the time she'll come back and amend her prayer—speaking off the cuff. She's learning that God is Someone to whom we can speak freely.

11.
Play Games to Teach Biblical Truths.

Our children's favorite Bible game is "This is God speaking." My husband and I role-play a situation our children might find themselves in, such as a friend asking them to lie for them. Near the end of the drama, Jim slips into the hallway around the corner so the children can't see him and says in a booming voice, "This is God speaking." He goes on to give the biblical answer to the drama we just acted out. The kids love hearing his "God voice," as they call it. When he returns to the living room, we act out the response, just as we'd acted out the problem. These dramas reinforce Bible truths far more than if we just talked about them.

12.
Teach Children That Prayer Is Not Just Asking God for a Bunch of Things.

Our Stephanie heard in junior church a jingle that says, in regard to praying to God, "Gimme, gimme, my name is Jimmy." She remembered the line until she got home one Sunday afternoon but didn't quite understand its meaning. I explained that some people think prayer is only for asking God to give them things. "They'll say, 'Please give me the money to buy this new car,' or 'Please give me healing,' or 'Please give me a good grade in school,'" I continued.

"How should we pray?" she asked, still confused.

"First of all, we need to think of prayer as a conversation with God," I told her. "Pretend He's sitting on the couch next to you and just talk to Him. Praise Him. Tell Him how much you love Him. Thank Him for listening to you and for sending Jesus to be your Savior. Ask Him to forgive you for messing up that week. Mention other people who need help, like your parents or brother or the teacher at school, anyone. Ask Him to show you how you can help those people. It's okay to ask God for help in school, and to get along with other people, and to protect you from harm, and guide you when you're lost. God wants to be in our daily lives. Does that make sense, sweetheart?" I asked her.

"Yes, Daddy." Her face broke out in a huge grin. "God's just like you, isn't he? He listens to me. He loves me just as much as you do and wants to help me. Right?"

"Absolutely."

13.
DEVELOP A FAMILY MISSION STATEMENT.

Our church just rewrote its mission statement—what it wanted to be to God, to its members, to the community. Soon after, my wife and I asked ourselves, why not have a family mission statement? One night around the dinner table, we posed this question to our four children: "What do you want our family to be?" We asked them what our family should be in relationship to God, to each other, and to our neighborhood. We talked about how to love each other, how to share responsibility for what needed doing, how to have fun, and how to respect each other's differences.

My wife typed our mission statement into the computer and printed it out in color. We have put it on the side of the refrigerator where we can always see it. It's helped our children to see that we want to be members of a cohesive group who depend on and appreciate each other.

14.
NATURE WALKS SPEAK ELOQUENTLY OF GOD'S CREATION.

Take devotions and a snack lunch to a favorite spot in the woods or a park. On the way have your child (and you) pick up natural artifacts for discussion. When you reach your destination, let the child tell what the article says about God—His creativity, power, cycle of life, sense of humor, care for us, and so on.

15.
BE SURE YOU'RE BEING THE EXAMPLE YOU THINK YOU ARE.

I'll tell you the truth: I thought I was a great dad. I made plenty of money. My family lived in a nice house in a safe neighborhood and always wore good clothes and had plenty to eat. We went to church. I believed in God. Thought I was a Christian and was teaching my children how to be Christians, too.

Then one day the roof caved in. My ten-year-old daughter, Tammy, got mad at me because I wouldn't let her spend the night with a friend. "You promised your mom this morning that you'd sweep the kitchen and feed the dog before dinner," I told her, "and you haven't. Yesterday you promised your brother he could use your bike to go to baseball practice, then you took it yourself when you wanted to go to the park with your friends. Promises are important to keep, Tammy."

She exploded and told me how I hadn't kept a lot of promises I'd made to her and my wife and her brother. She wasn't making them up. She reminded me of the time I didn't keep my promise to take them to the circus. I was too tired. There was a night I promised to be at a school play she was in. I had to work late. She had a long list, and it shocked me that she was keeping all this resentment in her head.

I took her in my arms and asked her to forgive me. I promised to do better. I'll never forget the look in her eyes: She didn't believe me. Later, I fell on my knees and asked the Lord to forgive me, too, and show me how to be the kind of Christian father my family needs. It won't happen overnight, I know, but my prayer is that in time my family will learn to trust me and know I am a man who keeps his promises.

16.
GIVE YOUR CHILDREN A VISION OF WHAT THEY CAN BECOME.

When I was growing up my father often said to me, "You'll never amount to anything." This devastated me and I believe kept me from achieving my potential. When I became a Christian, I decided my children would never hear such words in my home. Now I say to them, "You can become anything you want to, if you work hard enough and let the Lord help you."

17.
BE THERE WHEN YOUR CHILD ASKS A QUESTION.

My mother was always the one who took us to church. My daddy, then and now, had nothing to do with religion. Because of that, as a Christian father I want to be as open and transparent as I can possibly be. I want Jason to feel free to ask me anything at all about the Lord, knowing I won't explode or put him down or tell him he's stupid for asking.

One time not long after he'd given his heart to Jesus when he was eleven, Jason told me he'd messed up, done something he wasn't proud of. "But I asked Jesus to forgive me. He will, won't he, Dad?"

"Of course He will," I told him. That's what I'm here for, to be a guide for my boy.

18.
VARIETY IN DEVOTIONAL MATERIAL KEEPS A CHILD'S INTEREST HIGH.

Our Kimmy has a vivid imagination. It's not easy coming up with creative ways to teach her about God's love. To hold her interest, we change our devotional guides every few weeks. Of course, the Christian bookstores have plenty of material but our budget is limited. Consequently, we've worked out a plan so our Christian friends from church swap with us on a regular basis—their materials for ours. We now have four couples involved in this "library," and it keeps all our children entertained, motivated, and learning important biblical truths.

19.
TAKE ADVANTAGE OF YOUR CHILD'S NATURAL ACTING ABILITIES.

Kids are natural hams. They love to act, and they love to watch other children act. The old familiar game of charades is an entertaining way to present Bible verses and stories. Don't be afraid to act along with the youngsters. Children enjoy their parents' participation.

20.
LET YOUR CHILD KNOW BEING A CHRISTIAN IS MORE IMPORTANT THAN ANYTHING.

I've always told Emory, "I don't care what you do in life, just be a Christian and believe in God. Having God on your side will give you all the confidence you'll ever need. No matter what you do, you'll do well." It's a father's job to encourage his child and that's what I try to do with Emory.

21.
READ ALOUD TO YOUR CHILDREN FROM CHRISTIAN BOOKS.

Children love to hear their parents read, not just for what they're hearing, but because the parents are *there*, spending time with them, listening to them, maybe holding them on their laps, snuggling with them. Jennifer has a favorite Bible storybook that is falling apart at the spine. When she was little we read the stories to her. Now she's a good reader and enjoys reading the stories to us. We sit around the fire on a cold winter's night and read to each other. It doesn't get much better than that.

22.

QUESTION AND ANSWER GAMES TEACH IMPORTANT TRUTHS.

Write up dozens of questions about how Christians live for God, about temptations and how to handle them, about stories in the Bible. Every night after dinner, our girls, who are ten and eleven, draw out a question from a special tin box their grandmother gave them. We all try to think of a Scripture verse that answers the question or find the place in the Bible where the story is told.

23.

MAKE SCRIPTURE MEMORIZATION FUN.

We have a gumball machine in the kitchen that can be used only if one of the children says a Scripture verse from memory. Stephen and Sara have a stash of pennies, nickels, and dimes in their rooms. When they say a verse they may use one of their coins and receive a treat. When the machine is full, we give them their money back and the process starts over, or we choose to send the money to a missionary family. Receiving this little treat encourages them to learn verses that will stay with them their entire lives and guide them in the ways of the Lord.

24.

CREATE A LIVING CHRISTMAS STORY.

During the Christmas season we invite neighbors and friends to read the Christmas story from the Bible with us in our barn. Usually it's Christmas Eve. After the reading, we discuss the details: putting a newborn in the manger, general barn cleanliness, goats nibbling on clothing, sleeping on scratchy hay, no electricity. This helps us envision what sort of environment greeted our Lord when He was born into this world. It really brings life to the Bible account. Then we light candles and sing carols.

If you don't have a barn, you can use a garden shed, playhouse, or garage to get a feel for what that first Christmas might have been like.

Finicky Eating

We remember the fish which we ate freely in Egypt, the cucumbers, the melons, the leeks, the onions, and the garlic; but now our whole being is dried up; there is nothing at all except this manna before our eyes!

NUMBERS 11:5–6

Terry stared at the broccoli. He would not eat it.

Ken, my husband, put down his fork, gave Terry a stern look, and started telling a story the family had heard a hundred times.

"My mother couldn't get me to eat half the things on my plate," he lectured. "Then I went into the navy at eighteen. The ship I was on had no snack bar. I learned to eat what was put before me by closing my eyes and holding my nose, or I went hungry. When I went home on my first leave, my mother could not believe that I ate absolutely everything she gave me, without holding my nose and closing my eyes."

"But, Dad," Terry interrupted, "I hate broccoli. Even one of the presidents of the United States hated broccoli when he was in office."

"Eat up, boy, or I'm shipping you off to the navy."

Terry sighed and I knew exactly what he was thinking: *I'll never tell a story like that to my son. And I'll sure never join the navy either.*

1.
HE SHOULD BE TAUGHT, FROM AN EARLY AGE, TO EAT EVERY KIND OF FOOD PREPARED FOR MEALS.

No picking out certain items and shoving them to the side of the plate—that's what I teach my son. Mother dishes up the food, perhaps giving him less of what she knows he does not like, but he eats everything and doesn't fix himself a sandwich to fill up on if he doesn't like what was cooked. The starving-children-in-Asia story works well with some children.

2.
NEVER FORCE THEM TO EAT ANYTHING THEY DON'T LIKE.

Shelley is a finicky eater. So am I. I was forced to eat things I despised when I was growing up and I'll never do that to my girl. If she doesn't like what I fix, she can make her own supper. When we go to other people's houses, she ignores the things she doesn't like—*without comment or grumbling* or drawing attention to the fact.

3.
TRY IT. YOU'LL LIKE IT.

"Try it," I urge my boys. "One mouthful won't hurt you."

4.
NEW FOODS CALL FOR THREE MOUTHFULS.

When Caroline and John Kennedy were growing up, their governess reported they always had to take at least three mouthfuls of a new food before they could refuse to eat it. That rule works well with my girls, too.

5.
WE EAT WHAT'S ON THE TABLE. PERIOD.

I don't fix separate meals for each member of my family. If they don't like something, they don't have to eat it, with the exception of vegetables. No vegetables, no dessert.

6.
DON'T REMIND KIDS OF WHAT THEY DON'T LIKE.

"I hate green beans," Greg told me once.

"Okay, don't eat them," I agreed. But when we had them again in two weeks, I put a small portion on his plate and he ate them without comment.

7.
No Pressure.

Sara goes through cycles when she just isn't hungry so we don't pressure her to eat. She is not given dessert under any circumstances, however, unless she eats something of substance. We used to play a game where you had to take four bites of something before you could have dessert. It just didn't work and we didn't really want to enforce it, so I told my wife, "If she doesn't want to eat, fine."

8.
Don't Worry,
It's Just a Phase.

Josh totally puzzles me. Something he's liked for years he'll suddenly hate. I asked his teacher about his eating habits and she said all children do that. They dislike something for two weeks, then they'll go back to it. Perhaps a friend changes their minds.

9.
Don't Be Intimidated
By Threats of Throwing Up.

Our grandson, Jeremy, is a terrible eater, hardly liking a dozen different things. He's nine. When he comes to our house, being a grandmother and only having him for a week or so at a time, I fix mostly what he likes but inevitably there is something he gags on and acts like he's going to throw up if he's made to eat it. I am not intimidated when he pulls that stunt and I make him take at least a little of everything I fix. Mealtimes are not my favorite times with Jeremy.

10.
BE A GOOD EXAMPLE.

I make a real effort to introduce my children to many different kinds of food. Sometimes they are new foods to me as well as to them, but I try them, to be a good example. It's unrealistic to think we all will like everything, or even that everyone in one family will like the same things. My philosophy is, here it is, let's try it together.

11.
DON'T GIVE UP
AFTER ONE FAILURE.

Who knows why we like or dislike certain foods? If my family does not like something one time, then I wait a while and serve it again to see if it still is unacceptable. I have a fifty/fifty record. Half the foods get a "yes" the second time, and half of them are on the "no" list forever. Well, maybe not forever. There's next year. . .

12.
TRY DIFFERENT RECIPES
FOR THE SAME FOOD.

How many ways can one fix hamburger? I rest my case.

13.
TEACH YOUR CHILDREN
NOT TO MAKE UGLY SOUNDS
OF REJECTION OVER THEIR FOOD.

We had dinner last week with a friend of ours and her six-year-old daughter made the most awful, disgusting noises over certain foods she did not like. "I'm going to barf if I eat this," she whined. "It looks like _____[fill in the blank]." My friend just smiled and said nothing. I hope she spanked the child later, or at least had a firm talk with her; I certainly would have. My meal was far from enjoyable because of that child's nasty and ungrateful comments.

14.
TEACH A CHILD TO COOK
WHEN HE'S YOUNG.

Randall eats much better than he used to because he now helps me fix some meals. He's not so afraid to try things like fresh vegetables because he works with them in his hands and they aren't intimidating anymore.

15.
HELP YOUR CHILD TO UNDERSTAND
THAT COOKING FOR THEM
IS AN ACT OF LOVE.

When my two girls began refusing this and that, I nicely pointed out that cooking took a lot of my time, and that it was an act of my love for them. I wanted my efforts to be appreciated, just as they both wanted their schoolwork to be appreciated by their teachers. When I taught them to cook, they were quick to see that it does, indeed, take time to prepare a nice meal, and it is not enjoyable when someone will not even reward your efforts by taking one bite.

16.
TEACH CHILDREN TO PRAISE THE CHEF.

It's one thing to get children to eat a variety of things, and quite another to teach them to praise the efforts of the person preparing their food. They should not take for granted food set before them and should be taught to be thankful—to God and to their parents. Good manners begin at home, at the table.

17.
FORGET MAKING THEM EAT EVERYTHING ON THEIR PLATES.

Nutritionists have shown the error of making kids eat absolutely everything on their plates. Many of us grew up with that training, and grew "out" with it, too. The amount of food one eats is not nearly as important as what one eats. Start young by teaching children what is good for them, *and why*, and what is not good, *and why*. And the earlier the better so that good habits can be formed.

18.
LET KIDS PLAN MENUS.

Once a week we plan the menus as a family, sitting around the table. Each person is allowed to request what he or she would like and this way there is always something that appeals to one or more of us. The children accept encouragement to eat new foods because they know they will also have their favorites during the course of the week.

19.
SERVE A NEW FOOD WITH A WELL-LIKED ONE.

My son, Zachary, is hard to cook for, but I've discovered that if I serve a new food with another one he loves, he's in a better mood to experiment with the new.

20.
LET KIDS DECIDE THEIR OWN PORTIONS.

Finicky eating is not a problem in our house because we let the children decide how much of a food they want to eat. Because we respect their judgment, they respect our wishes to eat a variety of things.

21.
TEACH CHILDREN TO EAT MORE WHEN THEY ARE OUT.

When we are at home our children do not have to eat every food that is served, but when we go to friends' homes, or to a restaurant, they have learned to eat almost everything, if at all possible. We have trained them to be aware of the efforts friends have gone to on their behalf, and to not waste food in a restaurant that must be paid for whether or not we eat it.

22.
IF THEY'RE HEALTHY,
DON'T WORRY.

Brandon eats everything that isn't nailed down. Megan eats for three days and then practically fasts for the next three. As long as they're healthy, I let them pick and choose what and how much they want to eat. I put the food in front of them—the same thing the whole family is eating—and if they don't like it, they sit there with the rest of us through the meal, until everyone is finished and they can leave. I won't ever force my children to eat a particular food, but I do insist that we eat together.

23.
BE PATIENT AND
SET A GOOD EXAMPLE.

We have a foster child who is five. When Ryan first came to us he didn't eat very much. He said, "I don't like it," about nearly everything I cooked. We didn't force him to eat but hoped he would watch our other two children and follow their examples. During those first few weeks he added one food after another. Now he's eating like a horse.

Friends

A man who has friends must himself be friendly. . .

PROVERBS 18:24

My cousin's eleven-year-old daughter was caught shoplifting with a friend.

After the grocery store manager described the theft, Darlene exclaimed to her Allisa, "I can't believe that so-called friend of yours got you to steal those candy bars. Didn't I tell you she'd get you into trouble someday?"

Darlene had told me before that she thought Margy was a bad influence on Allisa.

But Allisa looked up at her mother with fire in her eyes. "Why do you always blame my friends when I do something wrong? I want you to know that I have a mind of my own, and my friends don't make me do what I don't want to do. I'm not the pure little angel you think I am. The next time I do something wrong, blame me, don't blame my friends."

We both shrank from her stinging words. The store manager just shook his head.

Later when Darlene had a chance to think over this reaction, she realized Allisa was right. "I was always quick to blame someone else for getting her into trouble," she told me on the phone. "And while I do believe she underestimates the influence her friends have on her, I greatly respect her courage in accepting blame for her own wrongdoing."

I agreed, and soon changed my thinking about a couple of my own children's friends.

1.
NOT WHO, BUT HOW
TO BE A FRIEND.

My wife spends time with our children explaining what a friend is: A friend helps another friend; a friend doesn't go with one person and make fun of another. Our nine-year-old daughter has a problem with this. Most of the neighborhood kids are younger than Emily and they vie for her attention. She realizes this and knows she is the kingpin. There's a tendency for her and one particular friend to disparage other friends and leave them out of activities.

2.
HELP YOUR CHILD TO LOOK
AT FRIENDS INDIVIDUALLY.

We have taught our daughter that it is not the number of friends one has, but the quality of the friendship. We help her evaluate the youngsters her age, to know which ones are good for her as a friend, and which are not. Sabrina has always had a lot of friends, and she loves being popular, but some of them were getting her into trouble at school. At first we just tried to get her to give them up, but she fought us on that until we took more time to explain the difference between good friends and bad friends. Now her judgment is pretty good, although we don't always agree with her choices.

3.
PAY CLOSE ATTENTION
TO YOUR CHILD'S FRIENDS.

We trusted our daughter's judgment in selecting her friends and she really made a mess of it, so much so that we had to move to another neighborhood to get her away from bad influences. Now we want to know who she is playing with, and we have them over to our house so we will know if they will be good for our daughter.

4.
YOU CAN'T ALWAYS CONTROL
YOUR CHILD'S CHOICE OF FRIENDS.

With one side of my mouth I say I want my child to pick his own friends; with the other, I want to do it myself, to be sure they're okay for Drew. But I know that when he is away from me, which is most of the day, he must decide on his own who is going to be his friend. That's why I talk with him about what to look for in a friend. Then, hard as it is, I have to trust his judgment and hope he won't be led astray.

5.
TELL YOUR CHILD HONESTLY
HOW YOU FEEL ABOUT HER FRIENDS.

I speak gently with Susanne about her friends and am honest about my opinion, but I'm careful not to put down her ability to choose a friend. I never say, "I don't like him because. . ." Instead, I say, "I wonder why he does that?" and often Susanne will agree and talk about it in a mature way. If I attack her friends, she becomes defensive because I am actually attacking her judgment.

6.
EVEN BAD FRIENDS CAN
BE A GOOD INFLUENCE.

Sometimes the bad behavior of Christopher's friends, and the trouble that follows, makes a far greater impression on our son than if we lectured him about his friends. Naturally, we worry that he will follow their example, but often he is stronger by refusing to be that way.

7.
BOYS IN THE HOUSE—NO.
GIRLS—YES.

We don't allow any boys in the house when our twelve-year-old, Debra, is home alone. It's all right for girls to come in, though. If Debra disobeys us, we put her on restriction, which means she stays in the house for a week and cannot use the telephone. She has just started to be on the phone constantly. When she is on restriction, she is not allowed to call or receive calls from her friends. During the first day of restriction she is allowed to explain to her friends that she will not be able to call them and they shouldn't call her for such and such a time.

8.
FRIENDS MUST MEET
YOUR STANDARDS.

It is a sad chore, but sometimes we have to keep our children from playing with certain other children. Our Krista is only four and all her friends are girls the same age or younger, except for one little boy who is five. He is more mature in his language and actions than the other children—and aggressive. He is too rough with the toys and tears up the house. We had to tell Krista that Jonathan cannot play in the house but it is okay for her to play with him in the yard and when they are riding their tricycles.

9.
BE CAREFUL OF THREESOMES.

My daughter, who is four, has two friends. One of the girls, Heather, is very quiet. She often gets the short end of it when our Clairis says, "I like Maria but I don't like you, Heather."

Interestingly enough, Clairis hates it when she is the one left out, and we use that as a learning experience to show her how Heather feels when she is not wanted. As much as possible, though, we let the girls solve their own personality disputes.

10.
BE PREPARED TO
HAVE YOUR CHILD SIDE WITH
HIS FRIEND INSTEAD OF YOU.

One of our daughters is a twin, and ever since she was born she has tried to get our attention. Finally, when she was twelve, she met this girl who, I can only say, is evil. We were very worried about our Kelly, but when we told her to stay away from this girl for such and such reasons, she sided with her friend and against us. Her friend has power. She can easily manipulate kids and probably will manipulate people as long as she lives. One day she got into serious trouble and this opened Kelly's eyes and she understood why we had wanted to protect her.

11.
EXPLAIN TO YOUR CHILDREN WHY YOU DON'T LIKE THEIR FRIENDS.

Rather than explain our feelings to our daughter we simply said, "Don't see her anymore. We don't like her." As we never gave Lee a reason why, she became more eager to defend her friend and her own choice to have her as a friend. We lost that battle, but one day we got smart and sat Lee down and explained in detail (calmly) exactly why we thought her friend was not a good influence on her. She resented it but took our advice because her friend was starting to get into trouble at school.

12.
STEER CHILDREN INTO GOOD ACTIVITIES TO AVOID BAD FRIENDS.

Gloria has many good friends, and one bad one. My wife has enrolled our daughter in Brownies, jazz dance, and swimming to keep her busy with friends who are nicer. On some weekends her special friend who lives across town comes and plays, leaving no time to play with the undesirable friend.

13.
BE A FRIEND TO SOMEONE WHO HAS NO FRIENDS.

There's one kid in our neighborhood nobody likes. When we see that no one is playing with Ethan, we'll say to our sons, "Find something you can do with Ethan."

"But he breaks everything," our Matthew complains.

"Ride around the block with him on your bikes," we suggest, but then Ethan will act up and we have to say, "Ethan, if you don't behave, you're going to have to go."

I don't think his parents ever enforce good behavior, but we do and, believe it or not, Ethan responds to limits and is gradually becoming a friend for our sons.

14.
GOOD ADVICE TEACHES RESPONSIBLE CHOICE OF FRIENDS.

I teach my children to be good citizens and abide by common sense. When we talk about their friends, I say, "I don't really think he is a good person. That's just my opinion. I don't know him as well as you do, though."

I always explain why I don't like a particular child for a friend of my son and daughter and this works better than trying to force a breakup in their friendship. Hopefully, good advice will create a basic image of what a good friend is.

15.
TREAT FRIENDS AS YOU WISH TO BE TREATED.

This is the advice I give my son, and Brandon has learned the hard way how bad it feels to be ill-treated by his friends.

16.
TRY TO STAY OUT
OF FRIENDS' QUARRELS.

Children fight and make up faster than we parents can whip up Jell-O. If you get involved in solving problems, you might make more of a mess than if you let the kids handle things themselves.

17.
"FRIENDS ARE NOT FRIENDS IF THEY
WANT TO GET YOU INTO TROUBLE,"
I TELL MY DAUGHTER.

Rachel got into trouble at school one day because the teacher told her to do one thing and a friend told her to do something else. Naturally, my daughter took her friend's advice. I explained that the teacher is like me, her mother, telling her what to do, and that sometimes so-called friends just like to see you get into trouble. "You have to learn who is the proper person to obey," I told Rachel.

18.
"LOOK AT YOUR FRIENDS
THROUGH OUR EYES,"
WE TELL OUR CHILDREN.

We never insist our daughters give up any of their friends. Rather, we talk with Jennifer and Janey and calmly point out why, in our eyes, so-and-so is not a good friend. We ask them to look at their friend through our eyes for a while and see what they think. Almost all the time they come around to our way of thinking.

19.
IT'S OKAY TO SAY NO
TO YOUR CHILD ABOUT FRIENDS.

You are responsible for your child's friends and have every right to say no to his being a friend to someone who is a bad influence. Our son became friends with a kid who was constantly in trouble: breaking windows, going to the bathroom in the bushes, throwing rocks at passing cars. We talked to Taylor about him but didn't forbid him from seeing his friend. The situation did not get better. We talked to Taylor again and warned him that he might end up in trouble, too.

He stayed away from his friend for a while, but then drifted back. Finally, when the other boy just did not change, we had to forbid Taylor from playing with him. Taylor obeyed us but still wanted to play with the boy. We were firm, though, and would not let him.

20.
BAD FRIENDS ARE LIKE
BAD FOOD.

One time when Danielle fought us over our not wanting her to play with a certain friend, we pointed out that we did not give her garbage to eat, which would be bad for her. "In the same way," we said, "friends can be like bad food. They can hurt you."

Danielle understood that analogy.

21.
HELP YOUR CHILD
NOT BE BOSSY.

We have a problem with our Stacy always wanting to be the boss in everything she does with her many friends. She wants to be the teacher, the top person. When we explain to her that she has to take turns, she fusses, and I must ask her friends to go home. She is finally learning that if she is not kind to her friends, they will not be her friends for long.

22.
AN ANSWERING MACHINE ALERTS FRIENDS TO PUNISHMENT.

I called a friend of mine once and the answering machine clicked on. Her daughter was speaking: "Hi, this is Brooke. I'm on restriction until May 30, so if this call is for me, don't bother to leave a message; I can't call you back, but I'll see you at school. But if this is for my mom or dad, you can start talking at the sound of the beep."

Manners

A word fitly spoken is like apples of gold in settings of silver.

PROVERBS 25:11

The crowded cafeteria line inched along. The delicious smell of roast beef, turkey, and fried chicken assaulted our senses and I could see a dazzling array of pies and cakes ahead. Ken's eyes were on the fresh fruit and corn bread. We were only four days into our scouting visit to the South to see if we wanted to live there, but one thing we'd already learned was that southerners love to eat—and eat well. Mmmm, can they ever cook!

We heard a child's voice behind us say, "Excuse me, sir."

Surprised at such a polite request, we turned and found a redheaded boy of about eight wanting to get by us. His family was up ahead, we assumed. He reminded us of one of our grandsons with his big blue eyes and chubby cheeks. "Excuse me, sir," he said again when we were slow to respond. After all, where we came from, I'm sorry to say, children did not address older people as "sir" and "ma'am." But we were learning that they do in the South.

Smiling, we moved aside, impressed with the boy whose good manners weren't the result of a nearby, prodding adult.

Since moving to Georgia we've come to know many parents who diligently teach their children such manners. One of the nicest customs is how southern children address their elders. They do not call me by my first name, Kathleen, but rather, as I am not their peer, they address me as Miss Kathleen (even though I am married).

Old-fashioned? Perhaps, but such behavior, such manners, is a sign of respect.

1.

MANNERS BEGIN AT HOME BUT END IN PUBLIC.

When our son complains about having to use good manners at home, and promises faithfully that when he is in public he won't forget, we remind him that how we act at home is how we act out in the world. Good manners need practice so they will become a part of us and not be something we must consciously remember each time we need them.

2.

HAVING MANNERS IS SIMPLY SHOWING COMMON COURTESY TO ANOTHER PERSON.

I don't frown on my children when they don't say please and thank you. I frown because it is a common courtesy to another person to say those things.

3.
CHILDREN MIMIC PARENTS.

It's simple: Parents with good manners will have children with good manners.

4.
GOOD MANNERS REQUIRE CONSTANT PRACTICE.

Sometimes Brittany will demand, "I want some ice cream." I just stare at her, without saying anything, until she remembers and says, "May I please have some ice cream?"

5.
GRANDPARENTS ARE GREAT TEACHERS.

My children had their first lesson in proper manners—saying please and thank you—from their grandparents. They take more advice and education from this wonderful man and woman than they do from us, their parents.

6.
NAG, NAG, NAG,
THEN TAKE AWAY THE COMPUTER.

Kaitlin ate with her mouth open. I nagged and nagged, but it did no good. Finally it reached a point where something concrete had to be done, so I said, "No computer tonight."
She screeched. She has several animal games she loves to play.
I wish I could say she changed miraculously overnight but she didn't.

Yet after many weeks, and more times when she wasn't allowed to play Zoo Tag, she finally began to make an effort to close that mouth. She's pretty good at remembering now. If the punishment does not involve deprivation for the child, it is of no value.

7.
ASK THE TEACHER FOR HELP.

Kalyn constantly interrupted grown-ups when they were talking, and though I reminded her of this discourtesy again and again, she never could or would remember. I wrote a note to her teacher at school, asking her to give a lesson on this matter, and received an "answer" that solved my problem. The teacher had the children act out a scene depicting such an incident.

The drama made such an impression on Kalyn that she excitedly told me about all about it when she got home from school. She has rarely interrupted again—just once or twice—but she knows it is wrong and now catches herself in midsentence.

8.
GOOD MANNERS MAKE
OTHER PEOPLE COMFORTABLE.

"If I chew with my mouth open, what's going to happen to me?" seven-year-old Tiffany asked.

"Nothing to you physically, but it will make people who are watching you uncomfortable."

"Why?"

"Because it doesn't look or sound nice."

Tiffany asked the same question when I taught her how to hold her fork properly and lay her napkin in her lap. Because she asks questions, I know she is really interested in the answers, so I take all the time she needs to explain every manners lesson.

9.
EMPHASIZE THAT HAVING GOOD MANNERS WINS APPROVAL.

Kerstin was bored by my lessons in manners. She didn't care whether she ate her food with her fork or her fingers, but when I pointed out that people liked being with children who had good manners, she quickly saw this as a way to win approval. Being accepted is as important to children as it is to grown-ups.

10.
BEGIN TRAINING EARLY.

The sooner a child is encouraged in proper behavior, both at home and away, the more likely such behavior will become commonplace. Treat manners as "something we do," and model proper behavior constantly before your children. Our son, Thad, has always been anxious to please us. Thus, he has picked up good behavior patterns by watching what we do and accepting what we say. We started training him when he was very little and simply did not let him have his way when it came to poor manners.

11.
DON'T GIVE UP OR GET LAZY.

Madeline tries our patience in many ways. She's ten. We rarely ask her to do something and she does it the first time. No, it's a battle. But we will not give up on good behavior and manners because to do that would give her the clear message that if she is ornery long enough, she can get away with acting any way she pleases.

12.
PRAISE YOUR CHILD WHEN
HE DISPLAYS GOOD MANNERS.

When Ben brings a friend of his into our house, he always introduces him or her to me and then goes one step further and throws in a comment to identify the person. "Mom, you ought to see Sandy on a skateboard. She's really the best." He never just says, "Mom, this is Sandy," and then we both stare at each other, say hi, and wonder what to say next. I have no idea where Ben picked up this behavior, but I thank that person from the bottom of my heart.

13.
POINT OUT BAD BEHAVIOR
TO YOUR CHILDREN.

This is easy to do in most families where there are cousins, nieces, and nephews. In restaurants, too, incidents will come up where a child is using atrocious manners and can be an illustration to your children. Seeing bad behavior is far more dramatic than having it explained, and when your children see how other people react to that behavior, it does make an impression.

14.
EMBARRASS YOUR CHILDREN
LIKE THEY EMBARRASS YOU.

I did a terrible thing a month ago. I had been unsuccessful in convincing my seven-year-old that manners were important. He thought it was "stupid stuff," and said, "Who's gonna care anyway? My friends act just like I do." What's to argue against that?

Then Brian "fell in love" with the new little girl next door and asked if she could come in the house and play. I said, "Of course. Would you like some lunch?"

Brian eagerly agreed and led his new friend to the table.

Without being asked, I joined them after serving sandwiches and freshly baked cookies. I had a sandwich, too, and as I ate it, I talked loudly and chewed at the same time, making slurpy noises. Brian frowned and kept glancing at Kiddra to see her reaction. Then I gave him the coup de grace: I slipped one of my shoes off and put my bare foot right up on the table while leaning back to eat a big cookie.

Choking, Brian yelled, "Mom, what are you doing?" But he's a smart kid. He knew exactly what I was doing.

Later, I apologized to him and explained my behavior to Kiddra who thought I was funny. Both children learned that just as they do not like being embarrassed by their parents, parents don't appreciate bad manners from them.

15.
MONKEY SEE,
MONKEY DO.

Kari was explaining to her little brother how to eat, what fork to use, and when and how to put the napkin down. He listened, then looked her in the eye and said, "You shouldn't talk with your mouth full."

16.
MAKE MANNERS
A GAME.

We play a game at the table: If you don't put your napkin in your lap by the time you take your first bite of food, you have to count backwards from twenty. I'm not sure why the kids get such a kick out of that but they do. We let them be buddies, or a team, to keep them from picking each other apart mercilessly, and my wife and I are a team.

They can help remind each other by poking and making faces, but if we catch them, they still have to pay the penalty. We have to pay, too, if we get caught, and it's amazing how we struggle to say our numbers backwards, the kids all the while screaming with delight.

If one of them gets caught with his elbow on the table, talking with food in his mouth, or chewing with his mouth open, then he doesn't get dessert.

17.
DON'T MAKE AN ENTIRE MEALTIME A LESSON IN MANNERS.

My husband comes from an English background where manners are terribly important, so he uses the dinner table to teach and remind, and badger and bully the girls into observing all the niceties. While his intentions are good, he creates tension for all of us, and this is not desirable when we are eating.

18.
USE GOOD MANNERS IN OTHERS TO TEACH THE CHILDREN.

We make it a game for the whole family to be on the lookout for people who show good manners. Once we saw a man hold the door open for a woman and she said, "Thank you," and he replied, "Oh, it's my pleasure."

Now our boys hold doors open, the girls always remember to say, "Thank you," and the boys answer, "Oh, it's my pleasure."

My husband told us, though, that many times when he opens a door for a woman, she neither smiles at him nor says thank you. We all agreed that such lack of manners is too bad.

We have now incorporated into our family manners the following exchange: A man said to another man, "How are you?" and the second man said, "Fine, thanks for asking." Now when we compliment each other, one of us may have occasion to say, "Fine, thanks for asking."

19.
GOOD MANNERS MEAN ACCEPTANCE AT THE TABLE.

If our children don't put their napkins in their laps before taking their first bite of food, they must go to their rooms and count to twenty-five before returning to a somewhat colder supper.

20.
MAKE MANNERS FUN.

Be creative in teaching children manners. Make them fun and not something that will be resented. Never belittle or put down a child when he forgets to use good manners. Encouragement teaches faster than criticism. Compliment lavishly.

21.
GOOD MANNERS MAKE SENSE.

On the Fourth of July, twenty-seven members of our family got together for an outdoor barbecue. Kids and grown-ups alike had a wonderful time eating fried chicken, potato salad, and ice-cold watermelon.

My Courtney, who is seven, was playing nicely with her nine cousins. Naturally, all of them were looking forward to the homemade ice cream.

But then something unpleasant happened. One of Courtney's cousins, who is four, refused to put a napkin in her lap when the ice cream was served, and she spilled a big blob of chocolate right down the middle of her pretty pink skirt, where the napkin would have been.

She screamed—actually, she screeched—and no amount of assurance from her harried mother that the stain could be washed out kept her from embarrassing everyone in her family.

Courtney, who does not always remember to put her napkin in her lap, sat there with her mouth open, watching this display. Later she said, "All that fuss over a little ice cream. Wasn't it silly? She should have used her napkin."

"Yes," I agreed, trying to hide my smile.

Messy Room

The hand of the diligent will rule, but the lazy man will be put to forced labor.

PROVERBS 12:24

A friend of mine at work was in a tizzy.

"My college roommate is coming for a visit," she told me, "and bringing her twelve-year-old daughter, Jenny, who is the same age as my Pamela Sue. The girls are going to share a room." Gerri rolled her eyes. "I dread the first time my friend and her daughter see Pamela's Sue's room."

"What do you mean?" I asked.

"If a bomb went off in that girl's room tonight, it wouldn't look any more messy than it does right now."

"Oh," I said.

"No matter what I say to encourage her to be neat, she isn't. No matter how often I nag, or even go ahead and straighten up myself, things never stay on the shelves where they should be, or in the drawers, or in the closet—"

"Where they should be," I finished the sentence for her, feeling a little sorry for Pamela Sue but not wanting to let Gerri know. Of course, I sympathized with Gerri, too. I had four children of my own and only one had a neat room. Enough said.

"The thing that worries me," Gerri went on, "is what Hatti will think of me when she sees Pamela Sue's room. In college I was a real slob. My half of the room I shared with her always looked a mess. She constantly teased me about it."

"She'll think she's back in college." I laughed. Gerri did not.

"I want to show her that I've learned to be neat."

"Gerri, every time I've been in your house, it's been that way."

"I guess, but I want her to think I've trained my daughter well. When she sees her room, though—"

"Gerri Hendricks," I scolded, "don't tell me you're seeking approval from Hetti based on Pamela Sue's room."

"Well. . ."

"Shame on you. Your friend is coming to see you, not a room."

"Yes, but she won't want her daughter staying in it, and I won't blame her. Who knows what lurks in those dark corners or under that bed!"

I was anxious for the weekend to pass so I could find out what happened. When Gerri walked into the office Monday morning, she took one look at my expectant face and burst out laughing.

"Tell me, tell me," I demanded to know.

Gerri wiped the tears from her eyes she'd shed laughing. "Hatti was so complimentary about my house, oohing and aahing over this and that."

"Yes?"

"Then when we all arrived at Pamela Sue's room, there was dead silence."

I started to feel bad for my friend. It must have been embarrassing for her. But she was still smiling. "Go on," I urged.

"Pamela Sue had done the impossible: She actually had cleaned and straightened her room. I thought I was in another house the first time I saw it. But when Hatti's daughter looked in, her eyes grew big, and later I overheard her say to Hatti, 'Mom, I'm afraid to touch anything in Pamela Sue's room, it's so neat. You know what a slob I am at home.'

"'Yes, I know, dear,' Hatti then answered with a sigh. 'Maybe you could take a lesson from Pamela Sue and her mother about how to keep your room neat.'

"'Yuck, who wants that? I could never find anything.' "

Gerri giggled and so did I.

1.
You Just Shut the Door.

I don't tell Carla to clean her bedroom. She has to live in it, I don't. The only thing I ask is that she give me the dirty clothes so I can wash them. I set a good example for her by keeping the rest of the house clean, including my bedroom, but there are usually a couple of days a week when it doesn't look as good as it should. So why should I expect perfection from her?

2.
Exact Instructions Work Better Than General Ones.

I used to tell Chelsea, who is five, "Clean your room, sweetheart." When I'd go to check on her fifteen minutes later, I'd find her standing in the middle of the room, confusion on her face, turning slowly round and round, not knowing what to do first. The task was overwhelming for her.

Now instead of giving such a general order, I say, "Put away your dollies, Chelsea." She knows her dolls go in two drawers of one of her dressers. When I say, "Put away your games, please," she goes right to the games and puts them in a cardboard box her daddy got for her. It's easy for her to clean her room when she knows exactly what to do.

3.
Carry Out All Threats— Immediately!

My sister was a pig. There's no other way to describe her when she was little. My mother moaned and groaned and nagged and cajoled and had a fit over her messy room, continually saying things like, "If you don't straighten up this room today, I'm going to dump your drawers all over the floor—not that that would make it look much worse in here."

My sister just acted bored and ignored Mom's threats.

Once I told Mother, "The next time you threaten her, *do it*. Take her drawers and throw the things on the floor; make her put everything away. She'll never respect your authority otherwise."

Finally Mom did what she threatened—three times. That's all it took to get my sister to start cooperating. Her room wasn't perfect, by any means, but at least you could enter without threat of bodily injury.

4.
HAVING A PLACE
FOR EVERYTHING HELPS.

In Mark's dresser there is one drawer where there are small boxes to hold his treasures: pennies, pencils, rubber bands, and little nails. On his desk he has a pen holder and a place to put his wallet and the things in his pocket, a place just like his dad has on his dresser.

5.
PICK THINGS UP
BEFORE BED.

I insist before John goes to bed that his room be picked up. I make him keep a path clear so if he has to get up in the middle of the night, he won't hurt himself getting to the door.

6.
SOMETIMES SHE JUST DOESN'T HAVE TIME TO KEEP HER ROOM CLEAN.

I work, and during the day Kelly is either at school or at the baby-sitter's. I don't get home at night until nearly six and by the time we eat and she clears the table and takes her bath and then reads or plays a few minutes, it's often too late to have her clean her room. Sometimes in the mornings she makes her bed and sometimes not. Most time-consuming chores must be done on the weekends.

7.
DON'T FORCE THEM TO DO THINGS IF THEY'RE IN A BAD MOOD OR TIRED.

Some days Destiny will come home from school and just be too tired or in a bad mood. I don't force her to clean her room then—but later is another story.

8.
A HORSE AND A HAMPER WORK WONDERS.

My mother just bought Lauren a clotheshorse and she now loves to hang her clothes on it. She also has her own hamper and she's very good about dropping her dirty clothes into it. At six, she's pretty good about putting her clothes either in the closet, on the horse, or in the hamper.

9.
CLEAN OUT SOME
OF THE COLLECTIONS YOURSELF.

Mary keeps every single piece of paper she gets from school until her dresser drawers are bulging. So, every once in a while, I clean it out. She knows I do this and seldom complains. I don't throw anything away that is important or worthwhile, but if she grumbles I just tell her, "Honey, if we saved all your papers, we'd have an apartmentful." She accepts that.

10.
A TOY NOT PUT AWAY
IS HIDDEN FOR A DAY.

If Andy wants to play with a certain toy, that toy must be put back when he finishes. If it isn't, we take the toy and hide it. He then looks for it but, of course, doesn't find it. The purpose in making him search is to reinforce that a toy left out is a toy lost. We return the toy to him after a day or so.

11.
PILE EVERYTHING THAT IS
ON THE FLOOR ON THE BED.

I use the excuse that I have to vacuum the floor, and then I pick up everything and pile it on my daughter's bed. Before Mindy can go to bed at night she either has to put everything away, or throw the pile on the floor again. Three guesses which happens most often!

12.
CLEAN UP BEFORE
THE FUN BEGINS.

"You can go outside as soon as you finish picking up your room." Ashley usually complies without any problem.

13.
WORRY IF KIDS
ARE TOO NEAT.

Mallory was painfully neat, really clean to a fault. As soon as she'd wake up, she'd start crawling around her bed straightening it up, making it perfect, before her feet even hit the floor. She wouldn't leave her room in the morning until it was just so. Before she went to sleep at night all of her clothes were put away. Her things were stored neatly. Her room was absolutcly spotless. This was before she was nine years old.

There would be times when we'd say, "Come on, Mallory, we have to go someplace," and she'd answer, "I will, just as soon as I finish cleaning my room."

She's eleven now and getting sloppier. We're glad.

14.
KIDS SHOULD CLEAN THEIR
ROOMS EVERY WEEK.

Every Saturday our kids wipe the fingerprints from the walls, dust the furniture, and vacuum the floors of their rooms. They don't go out to play until those tasks are done.

15.
A Two-Year-Old Is Not too Young to Pick Up His Own Toys.

I never asked Darren to put away his toys when he was two years old. I thought it would be too much pressure on him and would take away his joy of playing. Then we visited my elderly aunt. She was delighted to see Darren and pulled a basket of toys from a hall closet. "You may play with these, Darren," she told him. And he did, strewing the toys all around the living room.

When our visit was over, my aunt said to Darren, "It's time to put the toys away, Darren." Obediently, he scurried around the room. He not only put the toys back into the basket, he even pulled the container to the closet where it was to be stored. From the big smile on his face, there was no doubting how pleased he was with himself. That day I learned a lesson about "underexpectation."

16.
Set an Example.

We set an example of neatness in the rest of the house. Their room is their home. What they do in their rooms is personal to them. If they want the doors closed, the radio on, the windows shut, that's up to them. But keeping it clean is not a choice. It must be done.

17.
Help Her Be Messy—
Dump Everything on the Floor.

When my daughter was eight she didn't like to put her clothes away and left them scattered around the room where they easily got soiled and torn. One day while Nikki was at school I decided to help her fix her room the way she liked it. I took everything out of her closet and scattered all items on the floor. I dumped all five drawers from the dresser on the floor and on the bed.

When Nikki came home at two-thirty, the door to her room was closed. When she asked me why, I explained that from then on I was going to help her keep her room in the manner she liked best: messy.

She opened the door, saw the *huge* mess, and cried. But I was firm. I gave her the choice of either finding her room like that whenever I felt like it, or keeping things picked up. She worked until nine P.M., and her room has been nearly immaculate since.

18.
IT'S HIS RESPONSIBILITY.

It's really Jason's job to keep his things in order. He's ten. I make his bed and take care of his clothes, but as far as picking up his toys that he's left all over the room, well, that's his problem. They will lay there and I'll walk over them and mention this to him, but they can stay there for two weeks. I just won't pick them up. There are times that he likes to begin playing with something and will continue it the next day, so often there is a good reason for leaving something out.

19.
SHELVES WORK MIRACLES.

Krista had a big toy box filled with toys and invariably the one toy she wanted at a given time would be on the bottom of the box. Naturally, the other toys got tossed on the floor as a result of her searching. So I decided to put her toys out where she could see them, giving each one a place of its own.

We put up three cheap shelves, all low and easy for Krista to reach. Overnight she's become meticulous about where things go. Her coloring books, crayons, dolls, Tinkertoys—everything—has its place. And when she finishes using something, she puts it right back on the shelf in its exact place. I can't believe the transformation. Even though she's only four, she does a fine job. She has little baskets, too, on the shelves to house such small items as keys, pencils, beads, and so on.

20.
TAKE ADVANTAGE
OF VISITORS COMING.

On a day-to-day basis we just can't get our kids to keep their rooms straightened. However, when they're going to have a friend spend the night, or we're having company, they give their rooms a thorough cleaning, under protest, I must add. But every six months is better than never.

21.
AN ORGANIZED ROOM
IS EASIER TO CLEAN.

When I used to tell seven-year-old Katy to clean her room, she'd take forever to do it. Then I decided to give her organizational skills a boost. I got a big plastic laundry basket and told her, "This is where stuffed animals go." Her dad got a wooden bookcase at a garage sale and painted it the same blue as her room. "Put your books on this shelf," he explained to her. We got blue plastic hangers for her clothes. They are easier for her to handle than wire ones. Now that there's a definite place for each category of her possessions, it's easier for her to put things away. And she doesn't whine about not wanting to do it (well, not every time).

22.
WARN THEM WHEN YOU'RE GOING TO CLEAN UP.

At least twice a year I do a thorough cleaning of my two boys' rooms. I tell them, "This Saturday I'm cleaning your room. Anything that's not put away gets thrown away." I give them several days to be sure their treasures are safe, then I go in and make it liveable.

23.
SHOW THEM HOW TO USE A CLOTHES HAMPER.

My kids (and my husband) did not understand the function of a clothes hamper. They never lifted the lid and put the clothes in; they just piled the clothes on the hamper until there was so much on top the hamper fell over onto the floor and I could hardly get in.

One day I cornered my two boys and husband and said, in an excited voice, "I want to show you a brand-new invention." I made it sound so intriguing they followed me willingly into the laundry room. "Do you see this clothes hamper?" They nodded yes. "Look what it can do. It has a lid that opens. You just grasp the lid and lift it." By this time I was really excited; my family was not. They knew I'd lost my marbles. Today they are doing better about putting their clothes into the hamper.

24.
PUT CLEANLINESS IN PERSPECTIVE.

I don't sweat the little things. A messy room, while not my ideal way to have my child live, is a little thing compared to stealing, swearing, being disrespectful, doing poorly in school, getting into drugs. Those are the crisis areas of parenting. Of course, I try to show my children how to have a neat room, but if they don't, I don't sweat it.

Money

*Then he who had received the five talents went and traded
with them, and made another five talents. . . . His lord said to
him, "Well done, good and faithful servant; you were faithful
over a few things, I will make you ruler over many things.
Enter into the joy of your lord."*

Matthew 25:16, 21

"How much money can I have, Dad?" our ten-year-old David asked.

"Five thousand."

"All right. That should buy some good stock."

Ken took the play money, some gold-colored bills, out of the game
box and handed David five thousand dollars.

"What are you getting with it?" I asked.

"A hundred shares of Amcon."

"You're investing in a pharmaceutical company?"

"Yep. I've been reading in the Wall Street Journal that Amcon's
research department is working on a cure for a major disease."

"Well, it's your decision."

"Mom, how long do you think it will take me to double this money Dad just gave me?"

"As smart as you are, and as hard as you've been studying Wall Street the past six months, not long, I'd say."

And it wasn't. We had taught David to read the stock market reports because he was interested in our own investments, and then decided to give him play money and see what he could do. Every day he studied the various markets in the newspaper, listened to a channel on television that had nothing but investment news, and kept charts of the up-and-down movement of the stocks he had "purchased."

He did so well that when he was twelve he actually bought his first hundred shares of stock, with money he had earned working for neighbors. Our broker took no commission because he was intrigued with the idea of a youngster being so interested in the world of business.

David went on to get a degree in business and finance and still is interested in the stock market. We're glad we took his interest in money seriously.

1.

ALLOWANCES SHOULD BE
BASED ON NEED,
NOT AGE.

We never promised our children the same allowance at the same age. When our son was eight years old, he didn't need as much money as his older sister did at that age because she was in Brownies and another little club and had more expenses.

Periodically, with each child, we discuss his or her needs and, regardless of the age, try to meet those needs fairly. Of course, the children are still expected to budget carefully what they are given, and careless overspending does not mean we will automatically increase their allowance.

2.
Establish "Bounties" so They Can Earn Extra Money.

The allowances we give our three children are small and, of course, never enough for them. So we established bounties, or special chores different from the assigned ones, by which they can earn extra money. A list of these bounty chores is posted on the kitchen door and their value depends on the difficulty of the task: mow the lawn, wash the car, clean the windows, and so on.

3.
Give Them a Ledger Book.

My two daughters, ages eleven and twelve, were constantly coming to me for money for one thing or another.

To curtail such behavior I bought them each a ledger book and gave them a certain allowance per month. They were to record each expenditure. I hoped this would help them acquire some knowledge of the value of money and its use—and it did. Now that they have realized how difficult it is to budget a certain amount of money, they can understand the problems I'm faced with trying to balance a budget for the entire family. Today when I tell them I just don't have the money for something, they understand completely.

4.
Let the Family Council Decide.

We discuss allowances together as a family; each child gets to hear what the other is getting and why. In this way, there are no hard feelings about why someone is getting more than someone else.

5.

BE CAREFUL OF
OVERINDULGENT FATHERS.

When my son was seven his father and I were divorced. In the months that followed, Karl received far too much money from his dad. He got everything he wanted, whenever he wanted. He had so much money on him that his teachers at school would find loose bills in his desk and send the cash home in an envelope. He was totally careless and had no concept of what money meant.

I had a talk with his father and he agreed to stop giving Karl so much. I then told Karl that if he wanted anything extra, he would have to work for it. I gave him a list of chores I felt he should be doing and said I would pay him two dollars a week. If he wanted something that cost five dollars, he'd have to save, just like I have to do when I want something I can't afford at the moment.

This approach has worked miracles. Now Karl is more responsible about money and appreciates its buying power. I notice he works a little harder, too, when he particularly wants a certain game or toy.

6.

I GIVE THEM
WHAT THEY NEED.

I don't give my children allowances, but I do give them whatever they need. I don't think children should learn the heavy task of money management before they are in their teens. For Christmas and birthdays I tell them I will spend just so much, and then let them give me a choice of things they want. In this way, they don't expect more than I'm prepared to give.

7.
TEACH THEM EARLY THAT YOU AREN'T MADE OF MONEY.

It was my own fault that my children began to think I'm made of money. I am divorced from their mother and when they come to visit me, naturally I want to please them, and that usually means spending a lot of money either for eating out at fast-food places or buying them clothes or toys. When I finally began suggesting that they wait until they get home and let their mother purchase these things for them, they quickly answered, "Oh, no, we can't ask Mom. She never has any money." She is smart. I was dumb.

8.
HELP THEM SAVE BY GOING FIFTY/FIFTY.

I say to my boys, "If you want something badly enough, save your nickels and dimes and when you have half of the cost, I'll give you the other half." They can earn extra money by doing chores, and I've found if they really want something, they'll work and save toward it.

9.
GIVE THEM A BUDGET BOOK.

My daughter is twelve. For her birthday I gave her a red leather budget book with paper envelopes inside where she can keep her money. On the front of each envelope she has written the name of an expense category: entertainment, clothes, church, gifts, and so on. She is fascinated by the concept of putting a certain amount of her allowance into each envelope and watching that amount grow week by week.

I let her make the decisions on how to divide her money by herself, and I encourage her to talk to me about how the system is working. I am very proud of her increasing understanding of budgeting, and I let her know I respect her ability.

10.
SET UP A BANK ACCOUNT SYSTEM.

I keep 3- x 5-inch index cards in my purse with the name of each of our three children written at the top of individual cards. Any money the children earn is recorded under the column titled Deposits, and whatever money they spend goes under the Withdrawals column. All monies go through me. Because we don't give them an allowance, they have to earn their own money and, believe me, they're really little entrepreneurs. They do chores, work for the neighbors, and sell various money-making items. I then take the money and put it into their accounts by writing the amount on the cards.

11.
ALLOWANCES DON'T WORK.

Kerry came to me one day begging for an allowance because her friends all were given one. I agreed, but it was a disaster. She had the money spent each week before she got it, and then there was begging for more and more and more, plus promises like, "Mom, can I buy this with my allowance that I don't have yet, but I'll earn it by next Friday?"

Now I just use my judgment in giving her money for this and that.

12.
TEN PERCENT FOR TITHING;
TEN PERCENT FOR SAVINGS;
EIGHTY PERCENT FOR SPENDING.

My children each have three jars in which they keep their money. In one jar they put ten percent for tithing—this is the first money they set aside out of every amount they receive. Then there is ten percent for savings, and the rest is theirs to do with as they choose.

13.
ALLOWANCE AND CHORES
GO TOGETHER.

We give our eight- and nine-year-old sons four dollars a week for allowance but it is only given if their rooms are clean and their chores done.

14.
MATCH ALLOWANCE
TO CHORES.

If Noelle does only half her chores, then she only gets half her allowance. When this rule is enforced, it eliminates arguing because the child can be as responsible or irresponsible as she wants to be, knowing she will be hurt if she does not do all that is expected of her.

15.
BUY ONLY WHAT YOU THINK
IS NECESSARY;
THEY CAN BUY EXTRA THINGS.

This year Dallas wants two backpacks. I told him I am only going to get one but I have no objection to his getting the second one—if he pays for it with his own money, which he's now saving.

16.
I WILL MATCH ANY MONEY
HE EARNS BY HIMSELF.

I don't believe in paying a child to do chores. I tell my Seth, "Chores are what families do to make living together more pleasant. But if you earn any money by helping neighbors, or selling things for the church or Boy Scouts, then I will match it."

I never push him to work for others but I encourage his resourcefulness and drive.

17.
FIGURE OUT ALLOWANCE RAISES.

Once a year we have a meeting about allowances. Our daughters, who are eight and ten years old, present to their mother and me the amount of allowance they feel they'll need for the coming year and why. We listen carefully to what they say and never laugh, even when they want money for outlandish and foolish things. My wife and I take a few days to consider the girls' request. In this way they know we take their thoughts seriously, which we do. When we give our reasons for either granting their wish or giving them less, there is very little, if any, moaning or cajoling. Both girls get allowances based on their needs and the amounts are usually different—and fair. They have become quite skilled at negotiating since we started doing this a few years ago.

18.
GIVE ALLOWANCE RAISES
BASED ON YOUR SALARY INCREASE.

Once a year I get a salary increase at work. My son gets the same percent raise in his allowance at that time. He knows this will be based on his "performance" at home: doing his chores on time, being cooperative with his mother and me, and working hard on his schoolwork.

19.
WEEKLY ALLOWANCES WORK BETTER THAN MONTHLY ONES.

Since I only get paid once a month, I pay my household bills the same way. That's how Sarah used to get her allowance—by the month. But she was terrible at budgeting her expenses. Invariably, by the second or third week of the month she'd be at my knee begging for an advance or downright gift. Now I give her her allowance once a week, and she knows there is absolutely no advance allowed. At eleven years of age she's able to handle her money quite well that way.

20.
HELP THEM UNDERSTAND THAT MONEY ISN'T EVERYTHING.

When our daughter, Deanna, was nine, she was very conscious of the fact that she did not have as many "things" as several of her friends. She didn't make our lives miserable over this but she did question why some people are rich and others aren't. I explained to her that some parents can do things that make lots of money while others can't or don't want to.

While we were having a picnic in the park she amazed me with this observation. "Daddy, you're better than money," she said.

"What?" I said, not believing my ears.

She didn't hesitate in explaining. "Debby's daddy works two jobs and her mommy works, too. They're never home so Debby almost always has a baby-sitter. They live in a big house and Debby's clothes cost more than mine, but her mom and dad never have time to take her to the park."

Without shame, I admit I wept. It's sure nice for a dad to know he's worth more than money.

NEW FAMILY

*Now Israel loved Joseph more than all his children, because
he was the son of his old age. Also he made him a tunic of
many colors. But when his brothers saw that their father
loved him more than all his brothers, they hated him and
could not speak peaceably to him.*

GENESIS 37:3–4

It was moving day and our family was excited about the new house that
would soon be filled with all our things. We stood in the driveway,
assigning each of the four children boxes and belongings to carry inside.

One of the neighbors approached us. "Welcome to Cypress," he
greeted. He glanced at our blue van that had ribbons and pom-poms
tied from front to rear.

"Just married?" he queried, glancing at the four kids trooping inside
with much enthusiastic hooting and hollering.

"That's right," I said.

"Second marriage?"

"Right again."

I smiled when our second oldest boy, Jim, came over and said, "My room is gr-r-r-eat. It's got motorcycles on the wallpaper."

"I know," I said. "That's why we picked it for you."

The neighbor leaned back, crossed his arms over his chest, and carefully studied each of the kids as they came back for new instructions. "I have it figured out," he announced smugly.

"What?" I asked.

"Which kids belong to you, and which to him." He pointed to my husband, Ken.

"Oh? Tell us," I said as the four children gathered around.

"These two boys are yours," he said to me, "and that boy and girl are his."

We all laughed because he had it exactly the opposite.

"We're a family," I announced, grinning and hugging Ken's kids and my kids who were now "our" kids.

1.
WE ALL LIVE BY
THE SAME RULES HERE.

It's taking some time to teach my son and daughter, and Dave's two girls, that we are now a "blended" family and are all equal and live by the same rules. Since the marriage is still new, my children more often come to me to solve their problems and Dave's daughters go to him. Gradually, though, with love and patience, we are beginning to blend and weave the many strands of our lives together. The important lesson is that we are a family, and all live by the same rules.

2.
ENCOURAGE HIM TO BE
A BIG BROTHER.

My son resents the fact that a new baby is coming into our lives. He has friends who have had additions to their families and he's heard a lot of complaining from them as to how much trouble these infants are. Down deep, the real problem is that he thinks the baby will get more attention than he will and somehow be "better" than he is.

I encourage Justin to understand that the baby is going to be help-less, and will need a big brother to look after him. "Even when he's walk-ing and then goes to school," I tell Justin, "he'll always need his big brother to take care of him."

That idea so appeals to Justin, he's changed his attitude a hundred and eighty degrees and anxiously awaits the arrival so he can play his new role.

3.
DON'T FORGET THAT BIG SISTER
NEEDS ATTENTION, TOO.

When the new baby came, I spent as much time as I could with Sum-mer while Thomas was asleep.

4.
GIVE THE NEW PARENT FREE
REIN TO DISCIPLINE YOUR CHILD.

I have let my daughter get away with some things that her new father will not allow. It is hard for me to let him take over, but at the same time, I see the results of what he is doing and it's good. Even though it sometimes brings me to tears, or I have to say later to him in private, "Hey, I think you were too hard on her," I make myself take the time to stand back and watch how this is working out, before I get upset.

5.
A Child Has Only One Mother and One Father.

Perhaps there is too much emphasis given to accepting a "new" parent. Kids are put under pressure to feel this person is his mother or father, when he knows perfectly well he has only one real mother or father. Be sensitive.

6.
Beware of a Possessive Son.

If I have more than six dates with one man, my son becomes very possessive and critical. I try to limit the number of men my children meet.

7.
Don't Be Afraid to Set Limits.

My new wife has a fantastic personality that puts people at ease and causes them to like her almost immediately. This is what happened when my eleven-year-old daughter visited us for the first time since our marriage. However, one day she and my wife were grocery shopping together and my daughter really gave my wife a hard time about why she didn't have a shopping list, didn't stay within a budget, and on and on.

Teresa finally said, firmly but nicely, "Cindy, this is our way of life. We have enough money so that we don't need to budget. This is the way we prefer to do it. I know you don't budget at home either."

My daughter responded immediately with an apology and agreed it was none of her business. It was hard for Teresa to be firm but she needed to set the ground rules for the relationship.

8.
POINT OUT TO CHILD WHAT RESPONSIBILITIES HE HAS WITH THE NEW BABY.

It's important for a child to feel he has responsibilities toward the new baby. She will be a part of the family, and every person in the family takes care of the other members. I have taken time to explain to Brent that he can help me do certain things with Lauren: hold her while I fix supper, give her a bottle, talk to her in her crib, and make sure she is sleeping safely.

"And when she gets older," I say, "you can show her how to do things and explain why she shouldn't touch a hot stove or play out in the street." He likes playing big brother and he and his sister are developing a close relationship.

9.
GIVE PLENTY OF ATTENTION TO OTHER KIDS AS WELL AS THE NEW BABY.

When a visitor oohs and aahs over the new baby, we are sure to give older brother and sister some attention, too. Since I don't want them to feel left out, I fuss over them as well, bragging about their various accomplishments. When grandparents come we ask them to help us with this, too. As a result, we have had minimal jealousy over the adorable newcomer.

10.
BE SURE CHILDREN
UNDERSTAND THE NEW FAMILY.

By my first marriage I have three children who live with their mother. I married again and have another son, Joey. Every year my three children fly out to stay with me for a while, and one day I overheard my three-year-old Joey explain to one of his friends that his big brother lives on a plane. Why not? We pick him up at the airport and take him back to get on the plane. That's when I sat down with Joey and explained a few things to him about our family.

11.
LET HIM BE TEACHER.

Roger has taken it upon himself to teach his baby brother to talk and dress himself. The latter accomplishment just shocks us because we have always had trouble with Roger dressing himself. We guess he doesn't want his little brother to go through the hassles he's experienced.

12.
DON'T BE AFRAID TO
DELEGATE RESPONSIBILITY.

The first time my four-year-old son visited me and my new wife, even though he was only going to be there for two weeks, we gave him some responsibilities around the house. He was expected to help with the dishes, make his own bed every day, and do other little chores upon request. When he returned home, my first wife commented that he seemed more mature than when he'd left. At home he was not asked to do anything. I believe a child responds to responsibility and grows from the experience.

13.

BE AWARE OF YOUR CHILD'S FEARS OVER A SECOND MARRIAGE.

In a second marriage you may have to handle a child's fears that you'll get divorced from this mommy, too. Since I've started a new life as a Christian, I can now assure my eight-year-old son that this marriage will last forever. "I'm committed to Caroline," I tell him. We don't hide our arguments from him, so when I see concern on his face, I'm quick to inform him that these disagreements are not going to lead to divorce. I'm hoping my Christian example will convince him, too, that I'm committed not only to the Lord, but to Caroline.

14.

DON'T LET YOUR CHILDREN MEET YOUR DATES.

I never allowed my two children to see my dates because I didn't want them to form an attachment to someone who might not be in our lives for long. When I realized, however, that I was getting serious about Charles, I brought him into their lives slowly. We'd go to the park on Sundays, the four of us, and spend some good time together. They really liked that. Then he started coming over more and more and being with us at the house. We would sit around and talk or watch TV.

When I told the kids we had decided to get married, my son's first reaction was, "Oh, boy, what's the first baby going to be, a boy or a girl?" Then he went out and got a bunch of his friends to "come and meet my new daddy." I hadn't realized how anxious he was to have a father, or another brother or sister.

15.
MAKE SURE YOUR CHILDREN RESPECT YOUR NEW SPOUSE.

When Don and I got married we each brought two children into the new family. Naturally, the kids tried us out, to see how far we could be pushed into letting them get away with things. I was thrilled when Don told me he'd spoken to his two boys (who were giving us a discipline problem) and told them, "Don't think you can break up this marriage, because you won't. Carol and I agree on how we're going to raise you. We're a team, and the sooner you understand that and stop trying to play one against the other, the sooner there's going to be peace in this family." His sticking up for me to his children meant the world to me.

16.
DON'T TRY TO BE SUPER-STEPMOTHER.

You'll be lucky if you don't end up being the wicked stepmother! Remind yourself that you aren't a replacement, and tell your new children that you respect their need to love their mother and you aren't trying to take her place. I have my stepchildren call me by my first name so there won't be any pressure for them to call me Mom and then feel funny when they call their real mom that, too. "I'm just someone new in your life," I tell them, "and I'm here because your father has chosen me."

17.
REMEMBER THAT THERE WILL BE A DAY WHEN THE CHILDREN ARE GROWN AND GONE.

Whether the children are yours naturally or have come from a blended marriage, keep sight of the fact that eventually children do grow up and leave home. (When? When?) Be as patient as you can, loving, optimistic, and encouraging, both to the children and to your husband. Focus on the marriage and, if it's good, the children will have a proper atmosphere in which to grow. But don't forget the relationship with your spouse: Your husband will be around a lot longer than those kids.

18.
DON'T BE THEIR PAL.

I tried too hard to be a pal to my new family. My wife's three boys enjoyed this at first but then the waters got muddy. They didn't know when I was being their pal and when I was being their dad. It became difficult for me to discipline them, too, because I didn't want to hurt them. The first few times of tears and loud words were hard but they forged us into a real family. A father has to discipline his real sons, so why not his stepsons, too?

19.
HANG ON.

When I married Elizabeth her family resented it. Her first husband had died and they thought she had married too soon afterward. But we really love each other and the marriage is based on all the right reasons, mostly our mutual love of God and His Son, Jesus Christ. Unfortunately, a certain member of Elizabeth's family does all he can to undermine my position and authority with her three children. He encourages them to gripe to him about what I make them do around the house. He then sides with them, and when they come home they're rude and surly to me, and also to their mother. We finally have forbidden the boys to see that relative. It isn't easy to enforce but we see no other alternative to having our marriage and family attacked.

20.
EXPLAIN NEW RELATIONSHIPS
CAREFULLY TO CHILDREN.

My son was unhappy when my sister and her husband broke up. When she married again he was really confused. "Is Daddy Michael really Brian's daddy or is Daddy Bob Brian's daddy?" We took a lot of time to explain the new relationships.

21.
DO THE BEST
YOU CAN TO INCLUDE NEW MEMBERS.

When my brother married again, his new wife had several children. We explained to our kids that they now had stepcousins and we incorporated them into the family's activities as though they were regular cousins. Our kids accepted them well, although the older ones took longer than the younger ages to welcome them with open arms.

SASSINESS/SWEARING

A wholesome tongue is a tree of life. . .

PROVERBS 15:4

Ken and I were at Burger King with our four-year-old granddaughter, Janice, and there was a group of five little boys, ages four to six, I'd guess, who had had a birthday party outside. The remnants of their hamburgers and french fries littered many tables and had been squashed underfoot on the ground. Dirty napkins blew loose. While we saw no parents nearby, there was present an older girl of about ten, but she was doing nothing to control the youngsters.

When he noticed the boys starting to climb on top of the tables, Ken said in a nice, nonthreatening voice, "You'd better come down off there. People have to eat on those tables."

One blond boy of no more than four plopped his hands on his hips, stared right at Ken, and said, "You're not in charge here." He kept stomping.

I felt like jumping off my bench and telling him, "I'll show you who's in charge here."

He and the others ran away, laughing, but they all came back a minute later and shouted at us, "You're not in charge here! You're not in charge here!"

As Ken stood up to say something, so did our granddaughter. Janice walked right up to the boy and said, "Didn't your mother ever teach you not to be sassy?"

She had absolutely no fear of him; she just looked him right in the eye. As surprised as I was at Janice, I could hardly believe what happened next. The boy dropped his head, looked at the ground, and shifted his weight from one leg to the other.

"Say you're sorry to my grammy and grandpa," Janice insisted, now clearly in control.

The boy squinted at us and mumbled an apology. Then he and his friends ran off.

"That was very brave of you," I told Janice.

She didn't look at all impressed with herself. "My momma won't let me be sassy," she simply said.

"I'm glad," I said.

"She says Jesus wants me to talk nice."

"She's absolutely right."

"I talked nice to that boy, didn't I?"

"Yes, you did."

I gave her a big hug. So did Grandpa.

1.
Sassy Talk
Is Not Acceptable.

At school our daughter is the ideal child. The teacher goes on and on about how much Amanda cooperates and helps with everything. When I pick up Amanda after school, she gets in the car, smiles sweetly at the teacher, and waves good-bye. But after we're down the street she growls at me, "Take me to McDonald's."

I think her sassiness is an outlet: She doesn't mean to be unkind but she wants power.

"That is not a nice way to talk," I tell her. "I don't appreciate your attitude. No grown-up will either and you will not get what you want."

Amanda only speaks this way to me, never to her father, and I'm afraid this means I've allowed her to get away with sassing too often. I've tried to justify her behavior by thinking that if I stifle her too much, she will only exhibit some other more unattractive behavior. She's just feeling her oats, I have reasoned in the past, but her sassiness is getting worse and I feel her disrespect for me. Now I am correcting her <u>firmly</u>.

2.

CALL SASSINESS TO HER ATTENTION RIGHT AWAY.

When Elizabeth begins to sass me, I just tap on her cheek and she knows if she doesn't stop, there will be more serious punishment.

3.

RECORD WHAT HE SAYS.

I keep a tape recorder in the living room and am always threatening to record Matthew's sassy mouth. Unfortunately, he never speaks like that when he's near the microphone. If he could hear what he sounds like, I'm sure he wouldn't talk that way to me. When I get on him for sassing, he says, "I was just making a comment," to which I reply, "It's not what you say, but the <u>tone of your voice</u>."

4.

CHILDREN AREN'T THE ONLY ONES WITH SASSY MOUTHS.

Shelley was in the bedroom playing with her doll when I overheard her talking to that doll just the way I had talked to her that morning. The way Shelley mimicked me made me sound terrible. I was so ashamed of myself. *Is that really how I sound? No wonder Shelley talks back to me sometimes,* I thought sadly.

5.
I Allow Only
so Much Sassiness.

My son Larry has no brothers or sisters. For that reason, when he needs to let out his frustration on someone, that person is me. But I only take it up to a point and then I make him stop. "I am not your sister or playmate, I am your mother. You may not speak to me in that way," I say firmly. Interestingly, he never sasses his father.

6.
Sassiness May Be a Symptom of
Another Problem.

I really think Billy gets sassy with me because he wants me to punish him for something else he's done wrong that I don't know about yet. I explain to him as patiently as I can that I am his mother, I have lived many years longer than he has, and I won't accept a smart mouth. "You are not going to be eight years old forever," I tell him, "and the habits you are forming now will carry with you into your adult life. People do not like sassy adults."

7.
Is It Sassiness or Just Commentary?

Gregory is sassy because he always has an answer. I've explained to him that there are times when people speak to him when an answer is not expected. "You can smile or nod your head. You don't always have to answer with an alternative."

When I tell him to take a bath, he says, "I don't want to take a bath." When I tell him to get out of the tub, he answers, "I'm having fun."

All he needs to say to many of my requests is, "Okay, Dad," but he doesn't, and the perpetual arguing and commenting get on my nerves.

8.
Give More Love and Attention.

I feel children sass because they feel insecure. The way to prevent it is to stop it when it first starts, and give more attention, since those nasty words may just be a way of getting recognition from a parent.

9.
At Least Teach Kids to Apologize.

My daughter is pretty good at sassing, but she also knows how to apologize when she's gone too far.

She'll say, "Sorry, Dad." It's better than nothing, I figure, but she's getting worse as she's growing older. I should have broken her of this bad habit when she was little.

10.
Establish Your Own House Rules.

When Richie came home after visiting his father for two days, he was uncontrollable—just a brat—and especially sassy. I was afraid to say anything for fear of seeming to criticize his father. I tried to be patient and understanding until I just couldn't take such behavior anymore.

Finally, I sat Richie down and told him a few things: "I have no control over what you do or say at your father's house because that's between you and him when you're there. He has another life and another house. But when you're with me, under my roof, you will do and act as I see fit. There will be no more sassiness or naughty tricks like you've been pulling lately. Do you understand?"

He just looked at me with a yeah-yeah expression on his face.

After the very next visit he came back a demon again and made some particularly unkind remarks to me. Right away I grabbed his two cheeks with the fingers of one hand and squeezed them into his mouth. It hurt him, but for no longer than I continued to hold him. He knew it was his bad mouth I was not going to accept.

Since that day he has learned I mean business and, although I don't know how he acts at his father's, at home he isn't so high-strung after such visits.

11.
USE A DEMERIT SYSTEM TO PUNISH.

Any uncooperative spirit, neglected work, sassiness, or other bad behavior will earn my children a demerit. On the side of the refrigerator we have each child's name and a list of his and her demerits. There are three ways to work off a demerit: by being angelic and cooperative; by doing extra work around the house; and by having a privilege denied— one privilege equals one demerit.

For instance, if Janey asks to have a girlfriend spend the night, which she often does, all I have to say is, "Oh, Janey, you could except you have a demerit up there, so you can't." You'd be surprised how many hassles that eliminates once they get used to the system.

12.
SASSINESS IS NOT CUTE.

Parents make their big mistake in allowing a child to be sassy when they are very young. Instead of recognizing it as sassiness, a parent says, "Oh, isn't that cute? He's so independent." What they don't realize is that this child will still be saying "cute" things, only worse, when he is a teenager.

13.
SHOW YOUR CHILD
ANOTHER CHILD
WHO IS SASSY.

Once when we were buying groceries a little girl of five or so got mad at her mother for not buying the kind of cereal she wanted. While she didn't have a temper tantrum, she sassed her mother something good. It was awful to see a grown woman standing there taking this verbal abuse from a tiny child.

"What do you think of that girl?" I asked my son.

"She's a brat," he answered emphatically.

Our eyes met and I didn't even have to expand on the message behind his own admission.

14.
SASSING IS ANOTHER FORM OF
NAME-CALLING.

My son, James, occasionally called his sister a name like stupid. I told him not to do that but I wasn't forceful enough. Now he calls her names all the time. It's his favorite way to get at her because she's very sensitive and becomes upset easily. I know that calling a child a derogatory name long enough can imprint that connotation into his or her mind for life.

A child psychologist once told me to say this to my children: "Calling someone a name hurts his feelings, and we are not supposed to hurt other people. Besides, in our family, we want to build each other up, not tear them down."

It took some time, but James is being retrained to think of other less destructive ways to let his sister know he's unhappy with her.

15.
Don't Be Fooled By Innocuous Name-calling.

My daughter once called me a "doi-doi," which, translated, means a person who is a bumbler and not too bright (I had done something silly to make her laugh). The rest of the children began to call me that too but never in a harsh or rude way. It became a family joke on me, but one I didn't mind because I have a very healthy self-image and know how intelligent I am and adept at many things (in addition to being humble).

Imagine my surprise, many years later, to receive this letter of apology from my now twenty-five-year-old daughter: "I should never have called you a doi-doi, Mom. I didn't mean to hurt your feelings, and I knew you weren't really like that."

Even as a child she had known deep inside that name-calling, however innocuous, was still a way of putting down another person.

I thanked Dina for her apology and accepted it. I'm quite sure she will not allow any such name-calling when she has children of her own.

16.
Sassiness at Home Is the Worst Place.

My son often tells me, when I correct him for being sassy, that he only talks this way at home. "I never say things like that to my friends," he whines. This is supposed to make me realize how terrible our family is, and richly deserving of Kory's sharp tongue.

"When we are with our family," I have taught him, "we should be on our best behavior. They are the people we love more than anyone in the world. Yes, we can relax when we're together, but not to the point where we don't care if we treat each other unkindly."

17.
SWEARING IS NOT FUNNY.

Never laugh at a child's profanity and think it is cute. You may start a pattern of behavior that will be hard to break.

The first time I heard my daughter swear was when she was three years old. I came home from work, tired and cranky. I had barely set foot inside the door when up came Jenny and said, "G..d. . . it," with just the proper inflection.

It so caught me off-guard that instead of acting shocked, I burst out laughing—whereupon she repeated the phrase several more times! It was then almost impossible to tell her that she was saying a terrible thing, offending God, the Creator of the universe, after having received such a nice reaction from Daddy.

A week or so later it came up again, only this time when I told Jennifer that it was a bad thing to say such words, she replied, "Well then, it's not nice for you to say them either."

I was ashamed that she'd caught me using such language, a habit I wanted desperately to break. "Okay," I said, "from now on if you hear me say something you don't think is nice, you tell me about it. And I'll do the same for you."

Knowing my impressionable daughter was listening to my every word, I prayed to God to help me be a good example to her. And He did.

18.
SHOW BY EXAMPLE.

"There are lots of people in this world who don't swear," I said to my daughter. "Let's be two of them."

19.
Warn Them of Negative Feelings Toward Swearing and Sassiness.

"Many people do not like swearing and being sassy," I told my son, Kenny. "If we use bad words, others will think less of us."

20.
We Don't Have to Talk the Way Others Do.

Sydney doesn't swear, at least not in front of me, but she likes to tell me what her friends say. I get the idea that she thinks it's okay to use certain words if other people use them. Then I tell her, "I hear those same words at work, but that doesn't mean I have to say them, too. We don't have to be like other people if we don't want to."

21.
There Should Be Rules of Speech.

My son is three, and when he goes to my mom's house, he rarely sasses her or breaks the rules. When he asks to do something and she tells him no, he knows she means it and he accepts it. On the other hand, he sasses me, refuses to take no for an answer, whines, deliberately disobeys, and is downright obnoxious. The difference is, I've finally figured out, I let him dictate the rules. I plead and cajole him to behave. Mother just expects good behavior, and he responds to that, even at three.

SCHOOL

The fear of the LORD is the beginning of knowledge, but fools despise wisdom and instruction.

PROVERBS 1:7

"Hurry up, Jim, it's almost time for the news. Terry, are you out of bed yet?"

Every morning at seven o'clock when my husband and I watched the news, we had our children watch it, too. We wanted them to be knowledgeable of world and national events. But do you think they joined us willingly? No way. The little darlings fought us every single day. You'd think we were dastardly villains the way they complained.

"Seven o'clock is too early to be thinking," Jim would say.

"I don't have time to get ready," Terry would chant. Or we'd hear, "Other kids' parents don't make them watch the news. Why do I have to? . . . I don't understand what they're saying. . . This is a waste of time. . . I fall asleep in class because I have to get up so early. . . ."

"Ten minutes," my husband reminded them. "Ten minutes is all the sleep you're missing, all the time it's taking away from your getting ready."

I'd give him a look of encouragement.

When Jim brought home his report card there was a note from a teacher saying he contributed well to the class.

"What does this mean?" I questioned him.

He gave me a sheepish grin. "I'm the only one in the class who knows what's going on in the world. When the teacher asks questions, I usually know the answers."

Terry joined us at the table. "And today I was the only one in my room who knew how the Senate and House of Representatives voted on important bills."

There's more than one place to have school, I thought, as I tousled the hair of our bright children.

1.
HAVE A DEFINITE TIME EACH DAY FOR HOMEWORK.

We always let Jesse come home from school, have his snack, and play for a while. At an hour before dinner, it's time for homework. This way he has time first to relax after school and enjoy himself. After that, homework calms him down for dinner. When the meal is finished, he is free to watch TV or play on the computer.

2.
THE TV GOES OFF. SOFT MUSIC GOES ON.

That's how to get homework done.

3.
CHECK WITH TEACHERS
IF THERE'S A QUESTION.

Rob never had any homework. When we questioned him about this, he said he'd already done it. On a different occasion when we were talking to the teacher we found out that Rob never did his homework. Things changed from then on.

4.
DON'T MAKE KIDS
DO HOMEWORK
IMMEDIATELY AFTER SCHOOL.

When I come home from work I don't always feel like balancing my checkbook or writing a difficult letter. My children need time to relax and unwind, too. I simply have the rule that if there is homework, it is to be done before bedtime, otherwise there will be a restriction the next day. I don't tell them to turn off the TV, or to do assignments before supper, or set any rule as to when homework is to be done. I let them do what needs to be done when the mood is right for them. My only concern is that homework is done, not when.

5.
HAVE CHILDREN
HELP EACH OTHER.

If two children get along together, sharing knowledge can be a close and beautiful tie between them.

6.
Supplement Homework to Make It More Interesting.

Because Stephen wasn't doing his homework, his teacher suggested we have him do related things to make studying more interesting. We gave him a magazine, picked a topic that he liked and that was related to his schoolwork, and said, "Go through this magazine and pick out everything you can find about so-and-so."

As he got older, the research became more difficult, but not beyond what he could handle. In addition to the magazine or book, we purchased educational toys, a calculator just for him, and some educational but fun computer games.

7.
Give a Dollar for Every High Mark.

For every "O" (Outstanding) our daughter gets in school, we give her one dollar. She usually gets straight O's. When we first began this program we questioned whether it was wise, but then we thought of ourselves at our jobs. We know that if we do well in our work, we expect our paycheck to reflect our efforts. So we decided to reward our daughter for her hard work, too.

8.
Don't Pay for Grades Just Because Other Parents Do.

Our son, Adam, told us his best friend's parents pay him five dollars for every "A" he makes. Adam wanted his father and me to do the same. We said no. "We want you to learn because it's fun to learn, because it makes you feel good inside to know things. We don't always get paid for working hard." He didn't like our answer but we hope he'll understand someday.

9.
Don't Just Accept Poor Grades. There May Be a Reason for Such Marks.

When one of our daughter's teachers pointed out to us that Susy was not doing well in school, she was put into a remedial reading class. This move helped, but the grades did not get better. We dropped her back a year. Still no improvement. Finally, the school suggested she see a psychologist, which we agreed to, but that didn't help either.

The last thing we did, which should have been the first, was to see a doctor. There we found the answer: Susan had a perceptual problem called dyslexia. Her vision transposed the letters of a word so that she had great difficulty reading.

She has been taking special classes to correct this for three years, and what a difference! We should have given her a physical exam first. She has deep emotional scars from having been put back a year, which really wasn't necessary. Now that she knows what caused her difficulties in school, she is coming out of it, and the knowledge is giving her the courage to conquer her problem.

10.
You Can't Ever Lose a Good Education.

I tell my children, "You can lose your arm or your leg and be handicapped, but if you have a good mind, an educated mind, you can still work and be productive. These few years in school will determine how you spend the next sixty years of your life, so you'd better do a good job of learning."

11.
POOR GRADES
MEAN NO TELEVISION.

TV is Rhonda's devil. She watches television almost constantly. The threat of removing that source of pleasure will make her do almost anything—even study.

12.
TREAT EACH CHILD
AS AN INDIVIDUAL.

Our second oldest daughter was tested for MGM (mentally gifted minds) and the school decided to put her into special classes. Although the school informed us of this, someone forgot to counsel our daughter, Janice, as to exactly what these classes meant.

At home, although we were terribly pleased that she was gifted and had the opportunity to take advanced classes, we did not talk about her achievement for fear of hurting our oldest daughter who is a year and a half older and not in any MGM programs. Also, we were afraid too much attention paid to Janice's new classes might give her a swelled head.

She began doing poorly in her new classes, a fact we didn't learn until nearly the end of the school year. Part of the blame may be placed on her teacher's personal problems, but the main reason was far more devastating. Janice thought she was in a class for poor students and was so demoralized that she just couldn't do the work. Once she found out that she was in an MGM program, she snapped back into being a bright student again.

Next time any such situation arises, we will be sure to discuss it more thoroughly and help each child to understand her own gifts and problems.

13.
USE THE DINNER TABLE.

One reason our youngest child has tested very high in a number of general comprehension tests can likely be traced to the dinner table. There, over breakfast and dinner, his mother and I and his two older sisters talk about what is going on in the world. Discussing a variety of grown-up subjects stimulates his mind beyond cartoons and comic books.

14.
LET HIM DO
HIS OWN HOMEWORK.

I am not qualified to help Danny with his homework. Not only do I not understand some of the subject matter, but I do not know what approach his teacher is taking. If I were to help him, it might only confuse what the school is trying to teach him. I gladly support him, help him locate places where he can find the answers, and listen to him try to work things out, but my firm rule is this: He does his own homework.

15.
ENCOURAGE HIM
TO BE SOCIAL.

I think being socially well-adjusted at school has a tremendous effect upon a child's learning. If he's worried about who is going to play with him at recess, or if he has to eat lunch alone, it's going to hinder his learning. We pay close attention to his citizenship grades. With us, "Satisfactory" is okay. As long as he's satisfactory and average, I think that's fine. Sure, maybe he can be "Outstanding," but as long as he's comfortable where he's at, we're happy, too.

16.
PAY ATTENTION TO WHAT THEY'RE DOING IN SCHOOL.

I had problems with my nine-year-old daughter in school, mostly because of my recent divorce. Leslie developed behavior problems and began hitting other children and creating disturbances—anything to get attention. The teacher finally contacted me and I explained that Leslie was her daddy's girl, and all of a sudden Daddy was out of her life.

The teacher had suspected as much already. When she told her students, "Have your mommy or daddy help with this," Leslie would start to cry and say, "But my daddy doesn't live at home."

Now I make a gigantic effort to talk with her every single day about what she did in school. She has settled down some and her grades have improved, but it's taken time.

17.
EXPOSE THEM TO BOOKS, BOOKS, AND MORE BOOKS.

I firmly believe the reason our children have done so well in school is that from the time they were very small, we read them books over and over again, and gave them books to build up their own personal libraries. Eventually, they learned to read the books themselves, without even being taught. Cultivate early a love of books—and young minds will blossom.

18.
SHOW THEM THE ALTERNATIVE
TO A GOOD EDUCATION.

My twin boys idolized their older cousin, Toby, but for a while, that wasn't good.

When Toby turned seventeen, and my boys were ten, he knew everything there was to know about everything. He decided to drop out of school and get a job.

"School's a drag," he said. "It will be great to get a steady job and earn some money."

My boys heard him say this.

My brother, instead of fighting him, agreed to let him quit and even helped him get a job at a steel mill stoking the ovens during the summer months.

Come September, Toby was one of the first down at the high school to reenroll. He graduated that year, went on to college, got his bachelor's degree, his master's, his doctorate, and is now teaching mathematics at the University of Michigan. Once he found what a lack of education would mean—that about the best job he was ever going to get for the next forty-five to fifty years was shoveling coal and tapping steel—he decided it was better to sit in a school five or six hours a day and read and study.

His example had a profound influence for good on my two young boys as they grew up.

19.
HELP KIDS UNDERSTAND WHY
YOU DON'T CELEBRATE HALLOWEEN,
A BIG DAY AT MOST SCHOOLS.

We don't "do" Halloween. Because of its connection to satanic influences and bad behavior, we never decorate or get involved in its celebration. But at school they do, and Cathy came home this year frightened with the ghost stories and visions of blood and witches and scary places. She started having bad dreams and came into our bedroom several times a night, scared and wanting to be with us.

Although we explained to her why we do not celebrate Halloween, she is only six, so I know she didn't understand it all. She just knew that many of her friends dress up in scary costumes and go to haunted houses and she isn't allowed to. Not that she wants to, but she also doesn't want to be "different" from the other kids. I called her Sunday school teacher and asked if she could say something about it in class. She did, and it helped Cathy to hear a second explanation.

20.
GET INVOLVED AT SCHOOL— AND GET INFORMED.

I groaned when I got the yearly sign-up sheet from Mark's Home and School Association. *I don't have time to volunteer,* I told myself. *I work part-time. I teach Sunday school. I sing in the church choir.*

I volunteered, finally deciding it was the best way to understand Mark's school world. By going in two afternoons a week to help with special projects in Mark's class, I got to know his teacher, his friends, and other parents. It was a three-pronged advantage that gave my son and me plenty of common ground. We never ran out of things to talk about and he was proud to have his mom helping the teacher.

It's a good thing to help with your child's activities away from home.

Self-Esteem

Are not two sparrows sold for a copper coin? And not one of them falls to the ground apart from your Father's will. But the very hairs of your head are all numbered. Do not fear therefore; you are of more value than many sparrows.

MATTHEW 10:29–31

One of my best friends, Mary, who teaches elementary school, often tells me stories of certain memorable students.

If you had looked over the entire fifth grade of Hanover Grade School, Mary related once, you probably would not have noticed Emma Cartwright. Emma was a scrawny kid with stringy, dirty blond hair, string-bean arms and legs, and clothes that never quite fit or were in style. Yet she was a nice quiet girl who did her work neither outstandingly nor poorly. She was just there.

One day Mrs. Whitney, the school's music teacher, came into Emma's classroom. "I'm looking for a musician," she announced. "As you know, we have a fine school orchestra. My problem today, though, is that we have no percussionist."

"What's that?" a boy in the first row asked.

"Why, that's someone absolutely essential to any orchestra," Mrs. Whitney answered. "That person plays the drums, symbols, triangle, woodblocks, and other sound-making instruments. It's an exciting thing to do. Now, is there anyone who would like to try this? Don't worry if you've never played any of these instruments before. I'll teach you."

Several hands went up, and one by one the children went to the front of the room to be "tested" by Mrs. Whitney. With her tambourine she played simple rhythms that the children tried to duplicate. None did too well.

"A good sense of rhythm," Mrs. Whitney said, "is the essential requirement for a percussionist."

Mary noticed Emma sitting quietly, watching Mrs. Whitney walk down the aisles encouraging each child who wanted to shake the strange instrument. Mrs. Whitney stopped beside Emma.

"Would you like to try?" she asked her.

Emma shook her head no.

"Please," Mrs. Whitney persisted. "You've nothing to lose."

Emma stood up. Mary was a little surprised because Emma didn't like calling attention to herself. Still, she awkwardly walked to the front with the teacher. All the other students were watching her.

Mrs. Whitney tapped a few beats on her wrist then handed the instrument to Emma. She felt the skin and lightly touched the jingles. Mary was pretty sure she had never even touched a musical instrument before. Holding the tambourine almost tenderly, Emma moved her wrist slightly back and forth while hitting her hand gently.

"That's good, Emma," Mrs. Whitney complimented. "Let's try another."

This time the rhythm was more difficult but Emma's ear picked it up and easily translated it to the instrument.

Mrs. Whitney looked at the unimpressive girl a little closer and played again, this time a longer pattern and far more difficult. Again, Emma's imitation was flawless.

"Well," Mrs. Whitney proclaimed, "I think we've found our musician. Emma, please stay after school today and come to the auditorium for rehearsal. I'll teach you everything you need to know and arrange for drum lessons for you."

Mary said that Emma's eyes opened wide in amazement. Her family was poor and music lessons would have been impossible for them to afford. But this new opportunity was hers. Emma straightened her shoulders and looked around the classroom. The other children were staring at her—with admiration. They had never done that before.

"It was a different Emma who walked back to her desk," Mary told me. "Self-esteem was born in her that day."

"Did she play in the orchestra?" I asked Mary.

"Oh, yes. In fact, Mrs. Whitney taught her more than just percussion instruments. Today Emma is one of the most gifted solo cellists in the country. She plays for a famous symphony orchestra on the East Coast."

1.
IT'S SIMPLE: LISTEN.

Always listen when your child speaks, and give him your full attention. As a mother, I never realized that I did this until my own father complimented me once. "When David talks to you," he said, "you give him all your attention for as long as it takes him to finish. It's as though the whole world stops and nothing is more important to you at that moment than listening to what he is saying to you."

2.
LET HER DO THINGS FOR HERSELF.

I used to laugh and say it is because I am a lazy mother that I teach, or rather "allow," my child to learn to do things for herself. But the look on Cari's face the first time she tied a shoelace, or zipped her own jacket, or poured her own juice tells me I'm doing something right. She knows she has conquered something—she's done it all by herself —and each accomplishment is a building block toward a strong sense of self-esteem.

I even take time to teach the neighbor's kids how to dress themselves. I remember one little boy who was five years old and in kindergarten and couldn't put on his own winter boots. When I suggested that he try, he began to cry. It was a traumatic thing for him even to try. "My mommy always does it," he cried, with big tears running down his chubby face.

I could have spanked that mother! I gently showed him how to put a small plastic baggie over his shoe and then he was amazed at how easily his snow boot slipped on. That smile of surprise and wonder at this seemingly simple feat was reward enough for me.

3.
ENCOURAGE HER IN WHAT SHE LIKES TO DO.

Because Maria loves to cook I give her every opportunity to experiment in the kitchen. Such a creative outlet has given her a sense of self-worth.

4.
REINFORCE HIS EFFORTS, EVEN IF CRUDE.

A four-year-old cannot clean a room or make a cake or sweep the floor as well as you, but even though the result may be crude, the effort is what counts at that age. I encourage, then applaud, our son every time he makes the effort to do something worthwhile.

5.
DON'T INHIBIT.

Toni has been a ham since she was born. She loves to perform and our family encourages her. She feels comfortable in front of people and we make her feel as though we are genuinely interested in her accomplishments, which, of course, we are.

6.
LET THEM CHOOSE BETWEEN RIGHT AND WRONG.

When I reached an age where I understood right from wrong, my parents told me, "You do what you feel is right. We taught you the difference between right and wrong. Now it's up to you to make up your mind."

Nine times out of ten I knew what was wrong and wouldn't do it. Mom made it seem so simple to make up my own mind. I knew what she wanted and I had enough respect for her that that's what I did. Perhaps my parents had learned from my older brother and sister that telling them no just pushed them into rebellion.

This is a hard thing for parents to do, to let their children decide for themselves. Most of the time, with my own daughter, I want to do just the opposite.

7.
TEACH YOUR CHILD THE DIFFERENCE BETWEEN LOVE AND LIKE.

From the earliest days when we began to explain right and wrong behavior to our daughter, we tried to prepare her for the future. "You are our child, and we will always love you. But there will be times when you are naughty that we will not like you, or the things you are doing."

Once when she had been quite bad and was sitting in a corner for an hour, she looked sadly at me and said, "You don't like me, Daddy, do you?"

"Right at this moment, no, I don't like you."

"But you love me," she stated as a fact.

"Yes," I answered, "I love you." I wanted her to know she was loved no matter what.

"Does Jesus still love me when I'm bad?" she asked.

"Yes, He does, but He doesn't like the bad thing that you did."

"I think I won't be bad anymore," she declared.

I hugged her.

8.
Encourage Pride in Good Behavior.

It's important for a child to have good manners and know how to behave. Upon seeing a mother spank her little boy in a store, my seven-year-old James said, "Isn't it too bad that his mother hasn't taught him how to act?"

The maturity of his remark took me by surprise, but I reinforced it by saying, "Isn't it great that you do know how to act, James. I'm so proud of you." I let him know that I appreciate his manners, not only expect them.

9.
Knowledge Is Confidence.

When a person is knowledgeable, she moves more comfortably in the world. We've surrounded Tracy with good books from the time she was very small. When friends and relatives ask what to give Tracy for her birthday or Christmas, we suggest books. The influence of good books will last far longer than dolls, candy, or clothes.

10.
Never Talk Baby Talk.

Knowing how to speak correctly and properly gives a child a good feeling about himself. Before our first child was born, we were friends with a young couple, both of whom were teachers (later missionaries), who had a three-year-old boy. The vocabulary of that child was unbelievable and he spoke clearly and correctly. When we asked what they had done to accelerate his speech, the parents offered this explanation: "We have never talked baby talk with him. From the day he was born, we spoke normally, in an adult way. We call a refrigerator a refrigerator, not a ba-ba. We call water, water, not wa-wa or drinky-poo. When he begins to stumble in pronouncing a word correctly, we gently help him so he learns how to say it properly."

Taking their advice, my husband and I reared our children the same way, and they are both articulate and speak English beautifully.

11.

RESPECT THE CHILD
FOR BEING
THE AGE HE IS.

I was never his age. Oh, yes, I was chronologically that age years ago, but that was in a different era, a different economy, a different culture with different mores and different peer group pressures. I was never ten years old in the 1990s. It's a different world, and for me to try to transfer all my beliefs and philosophies of what I did when I was ten years old onto him is wrong.

12.

DON'T TAKE OVER
WHEN HE'S FUMBLING.

I get aggravated with my wife because she often finishes what one of our kids starts. She explains, "I'd rather just do it myself."

"How else can our children learn but through trial and error?" I say to her. "What's a messy kitchen or garage compared with the valuable lessons our kids are learning by doing things for themselves?"

13.
Fuss Over Their Efforts.

Whenever the children bring things home from school or church, we are sure to notice them and, not only that, fuss over them. We put papers on the refrigerator with magnets. Every day when I come home from work, I'll ask the children what they did in school and I'll sit and listen carefully to each explanation to let them know I really am interested.

14.
Listen to Your Babies.

Our son is only two and, although he doesn't talk in sentences yet, he talks to me a lot, especially while I'm shaving in the morning. He goes on and on and really believes he's communicating with me. I listen and nod my head, even though I have no idea most of the time what he's saying. But he gets very excited about our little "talks" and appreciates my listening to him.

15.
Teach Kids
to Be Competitive.

Being competitive is not a bad thing. It brings many rewards—inner as well as outer. I want my kids to be winners, not losers, not necessarily for the material goodies but for that inner self-confidence that comes only from being number one, or close to it.

I teach my kids to give everything they do their best shot. In addition to competing against other kids, I teach them to compete against themselves—the last record they set, the last goal they achieved. How about going a little higher, or doing a little more? In the same vein, I also teach them to accept defeat but never to give in to it.

16.
PRETTY ON THE INSIDE
IS PRETTY ON THE OUTSIDE.

Why do we work so hard to keep our kids clean on the outside and then expose them to filthy movies, television, and books? Doesn't make sense. This goes for boys as well as girls.

17.
REPEAT A MILLION TIMES
TO YOUR CHILD
THAT HE IS SPECIAL.

"Always think of yourself that way," I tell him. "Even if you get a bad grade or do something wrong, you are still special and I'll continue to love you, no matter what. If you think well of yourself, this will show through and then other people will think well of you, too."

18.
GIVE THEM
ANY KIND OF LESSONS.

Because our daughter likes music and we wanted to give her something in which to excel, she has taken cello and piano lessons for a number of years. Her accomplishments in music have given her a real poise and self-confidence that one doesn't get by watching television four hours a day.

19.
FORCE THEM, IF NEED BE, TO DO SOMETHING, ANYTHING, THAT WILL MAKE THEM FEEL GOOD ABOUT THEMSELVES.

Our son has always shown a high degree of interest in sports and has played soccer, basketball, and baseball. This year, though, he decided he didn't want to play baseball. When I asked him why, he said he wasn't good enough.

I couldn't accept that because I had watched him play and felt he was at least average, if not a little above. His coaches also thought he had potential, which they told him, and me.

So, I said to him, "You're as good as at least half the boys on the team," and I forced him to sign up.

All the way to the first practice he grumbled. If he had said he just wasn't interested anymore, I probably would have let him quit. But to say he wasn't good enough smacked of a bad mental image that I did not want to foster.

Now after only a month of practicing, and getting to know the other kids on the team, he is really enjoying baseball and doing very well. I'm glad I forced him, and so is he.

20.
TEACH HIM TO BE PROUD OF HIS EFFORTS.

When my son made the all-star team for baseball, I told him how proud I was of his accomplishments, and that he should be proud of himself, too.

"Remember how you went to all your practices without anyone telling you?" I reminded him. "I appreciated that, and the team appreciated it, and so did the coaches."

However, his ultimate reward should be in knowing that he tried as hard as he could. Even if he hadn't made the all-star team, he still did his best. He had a right to be proud of himself.

Temper Tantrums

A stone is heavy and sand is weighty, but a fool's wrath is heavier than both of them. Wrath is cruel and anger a torrent...

Proverbs 27:3–4

"I don't want to stay here anymore. I want to go home." Five-year-old Doug grabbed his mother's arm, spilling coffee from the cup she was holding. The scene was a committee meeting for hospital volunteers and my friend, Amy, hadn't been able to find a baby-sitter for Doug.

Patiently, she leaned down to him and whispered, "Yes, dear, we'll leave in a few minutes."

"That's what you said before," Doug whined, "and we're still here. I want to go *now!*" His little voice pierced the room.

"Dougy, sweetheart, if you don't keep your voice down, we can't hear the woman who's speaking."

"I don't care. There aren't any kids to play with here. If you don't take me home now, I'm going to be sick all over this chair."

"Doug," his mother said firmly, "you will behave yourself or I'll have to spank you."

"Oh, yeah? I dare you. Go ahead, spank me in front of all these people. Go on, go on!" he yelled.

Others in the room now turned to see who was causing the commotion. The speaker put down her notes. I lowered my eyes.

"Is anything the matter?" one of the board members asked Amy, coming over to us. She smiled. "Would you like some cookies?" she asked Doug. "The rest of us are going to have some in a few minutes but you can have yours now." She held out a plate of fancy cookies for Doug to see.

With a pout distorting his little mouth, he swung his arm and sent the dish flying. The china plate landed with a crash on the tile floor and broke into a dozen pieces. The other women present gasped, as did I.

"I don't want your crummy old cookies!" Doug yelled. "I want to go home!"

"Dougy, please," Amy pleaded.

"I'll break other things," he threatened.

Amy looked at me and I nodded my head. If she had to leave, we'd leave. Suddenly, I wished I had driven myself so I wouldn't have to miss the meeting, which was an important one.

"All right, all right," Amy said, agreeing to Doug's blackmail. She hurried him out after a quick apology to the group.

Once in the car, she said, "Douglas, why did you act so horrid in there? You were a very naughty boy, you know." She gently tousled his hair. "Don't be mad at Mommy for taking you to the meeting. I thought there would be other children there for you."

I saw Doug relax in the seat. It was easy to tell he was congratulating himself. No doubt he was thinking, *That was great. Everyone was looking at me. I'll have to do it again real soon.*

1.
DON'T ACKNOWLEDGE THE TANTRUM.

Anne was having a real leg-kicking temper tantrum in the middle of our kitchen floor. Both my wife and I left the room, deliberately stepping over her. We did not even acknowledge that she was having a tantrum. When there's no one to watch, the tantrum isn't nearly as enjoyable for the child.

2.
DON'T GIVE IN TO CRYING.

When Renee was not yet two, she started screaming in her room. After investigating to be sure nothing was physically wrong, we realized she was only attempting to stay up later. We left the room, and even though she continued to cry for a long time, we did not give in, nearly impossible though it was. She has never had another crying tantrum.

3.
A GOOD SPANKING DOES WONDERS.

I don't like to spank our daughter but sometimes that's the last resort. When she was about three, Jenny had a temper tantrum in a naval commissary. I took her out to the car and spanked her hard on her leg because she had lots of clothes on. She cried, of course, but she also knew I would not tolerate bad behavior. She has never had another tantrum.

4.
NEVER REWARD
A TANTRUM.

Don't give the child candy or make a good promise just to keep him quiet. He'll use it as a club over your head the next time he wants his way.

5.
GENTLY MIMIC
HIS POUTINESS.

Sometimes a child will laugh at his own poutiness if you act or speak as he is doing. This should not be done as ridicule but rather, gentle mimicking. If he is really angry, don't try this.

6.
DON'T FORCE HIM TO PICK UP
AFTER HIS TANTRUM UNTIL
HE'S CALMED DOWN.

There was a great commotion coming from Keith's room and when I opened the door he was throwing blocks all over the place. I told him he couldn't act like that. Did no good.

"You're going to wreck your room," I said sternly.

"Who cares?" he shouted back, but then he said, "I hate blocks. I can't build with them. This doesn't look like it's supposed to." He pointed at something indistinguishable.

I told him that sometimes I feel like that when things don't go as I want. "Forget the blocks for a while," I said. "Let's go get some ice cream."

By the time we ate a cone and got back to the house, Keith was calmed down and picked up the mess he had made without my even telling him to. If I had said instead, "Now you pick those things up, every last one of them, and don't you come out of your room until you do," he'd be in there still.

Why punish a child at a time like that? He'd had it—with *everything*.

7.
LEARN WHAT
IS CAUSING THE TANTRUM.

Our son is a mentally gifted child who had temper tantrums from the time he was two months old until he was in first grade. He would lie on the floor and kick and scream. He hit his head against the wall. He threw toys across the room.

After trying the usual methods, we finally discovered that he was having tantrums because he was frustrated. Being mentally ahead of what his body could do made him angry, and he'd have a tantrum.

We were helped to understand this when we enrolled him in a Montessori school. One day we watched him trying to put together a jigsaw puzzle with very small pieces. He was good at puzzles, mentally, but he was just not able to coordinate the small pieces of this particular one. He angrily threw the pieces across the floor.

My tendency would have been to scold him and make him pick up the puzzle pieces but the teacher didn't do that. Instead, she went to him and helped him choose a puzzle with larger pieces, which he mastered in time and felt good about doing. Eventually, he picked up the other pieces on his own.

Of course, it takes time and patience to discover how to turn a tantrum into something productive. Once we decided on this course of action, it was easier to handle situations that brought on a tantrum— like not being able to fasten his shoelaces. Instead of getting angry with him over the tantrum, we stayed with him and helped him learn the skill or worked in another direction, as with the puzzle. We also bought educational toys that helped keep him occupied and challenged.

At the school we were counseled to *never reprimand a tantrum*, for there has to be a basic reason why a child has one. Also, *don't ignore the tantrum*, but explain it to him while it is fresh in his mind.

8.
Don't Punish Again
If She's Had
a Tantrum Somewhere Else.

During a temper tantrum at school, Maggie ended up on the floor kicking and crying. She'd never had a tantrum at school and she felt so guilty about it that when she got home she wanted to tell me, only she was afraid to. I told her, "Please let me know what happened in school today. If you were naughty and were already punished, then I surely won't punish you again." And I didn't.

9.
If a Tantrum Happens in Public,
Simply Take the Child Away.

When our daughter was four we were eating in a nice restaurant and she got very angry and started crying. We asked her to stop but she only became more belligerent and loud. Finally we said, "If you do not stop crying, we will have to go home without finishing our meal and we will not take you to a restaurant with us for a long time."

She did not stop, so we left, much to the puzzlement of the waitress who saw our half-eaten food. We went home and had pizza, which punished us as well as Carol, but she learned that we meant business.

We made it a point to go to dinner again in a few weeks but we left Carol home. Remember that originally we did not say we would never take her with us again, for certainly we would want to. What we said was, "for a long time." In this way, we carried out the punishment for the tantrum, but allowed Carol to show us in the future that she could behave in public and, therefore, could go with us.

10.

NEVER REWARD A TANTRUM
BY GIVING THE CHILD YOUR ATTENTION.

If you reward a tantrum by being attentive and loving, then the child concludes, "Hey, this is a fun thing. If I lie on the floor and kick my legs and scream, Mommy will come and hold me and give me lots of attention."

11.

THE PROBLEM MAY BE
MORE SERIOUS THAN
A TEMPER TANTRUM.

When Gina was three years old, we knew there was something wrong with her but we couldn't put our finger on it. By the time she was four, and in preschool, the problems became severe and the teacher talked to us.

"Gina has social problems," we were told. "She doesn't know how to get along with the other children. Sometimes she's aggressive but other times she smothers them with friendliness. She doesn't know how to take turns or share, and she also has a problem with space: She bumps into things a lot."

My husband and I were distraught. We could add to these symptoms her behavior problems at home which included being very negative. Nothing pleased her. No matter how we did something, she wanted it done another way.

After taking Gina to a psychologist to have her tested, we discovered she had tendencies toward hyperactivity. Such symptoms as impulsiveness (doing things without thinking of consequences), extreme moodiness, and high distractibility are indicative of this condition. The psychologist didn't know if she would have learning disabilities because that cannot be determined until a child is seven or so, but now that Gina has reached that age, she does indeed have those problems, too.

Gina now has been diagnosed as demonstrating attention deficit disorder—ADD, which might or might not be coupled with hyperactivity. Many children who are not hyperactive can't concentrate and focus on one thing. They may need medication to help them in school so they're not so distracted.

By the time Gina was in kindergarten, we had learned that she had sensory integration dysfunction. By first grade she was diagnosed with multiple learning disabilities. All of these dysfunctions are too involved to go into but it has been traumatic for our whole family.

Through the years we've found support groups and attended all kinds of parent training classes to find out how to help Gina, how to cope with the trying situation, and what our rights are in the public school system.

How I wish Gina's problem had been simple temper tantrums!

12.
NEVER STOP A TANTRUM IN THE MIDDLE.

We used to physically stop the tantrum right in the middle and then sit down and ask why he was having such a fit. Every single time, as soon as we stopped the tantrum, Bobby couldn't remember what he was angry about. Such a strategy didn't help us prevent further tantrums.

13.
DON'T GIVE HIM WHAT HE WANTS.

If you give him what he wants, he'll use it as a weapon against you. Brad was having a tantrum because he didn't want to eat. So we said, "All right, don't eat."

From then on he had tantrums so he wouldn't have to eat. We stopped saying that.

14.
SEND HIM AWAY FROM PEOPLE TO HAVE HIS TANTRUM ALONE.

At first we used to leave the room when Joey had a tantrum, and this worked pretty well. But after a while we decided it wasn't fair for us to leave what we were doing, so we sent him away. "If you want to throw a temper tantrum," we told Joey, "please do it over there or in your room where we won't have to watch you."

The minute the next tantrum would start we'd say, "Would you like to continue that somewhere else?" It took almost a year of treating the problem in this way but the tantrums occurred less and less frequently and then disappeared altogether. We took a family counseling course during that time and it was suggested that parents give a "nonaudience response" to a temper tantrum.

15.
TRY A COLD SHOWER, WITH THEIR CLOTHES ON.

Only one of my children had temper tantrums, and these occurred at the age of four. Kindra kicked and screamed and held her breath. I tried everything to no avail, until my stepmother suggested putting her into the shower, clothes and all, and turning on the cold water. I did it twice and Kindra never had another tantrum. It's a super cure and doesn't hurt a bit.

16.
A Cup of Water
in the Face
Takes Away the Anger.

When my son had tantrums, I'd just throw a cup of water in his face—not violently, but right in the face (like we sometimes have to do when two dogs are fighting). This was such a shock, he forgot what he was mad about.

17.
Show Your Child Another
Child Having a Tantrum.

While we were eating dinner in a fast-food restaurant with our two children, we couldn't help but notice a child of about seven at a nearby table who was really mouthing off to his mother, and getting louder and louder. I said to my kids, "What does that sound like? Good or bad?"

"Bad!" they both agreed and meant it. It was easy to see how awful it looked and sounded when someone else was having a tantrum. It was a good lesson for my daughters.

18.
He Goes to His Room
Until He (and we) Calm Down.

By enforcing a time of winding down and getting control of himself again (which can be from ten minutes to two hours), we've kept disasters from happening. When Daniel has calmed down, we talk. Sometimes by then he can readily see what made him so angry and we can deal with it, and other times he can't. However, since he's no longer furious and beyond reason, he's more amenable to listening to why we think he was angry in the first place.

19.
HANDLE IT
RIGHT ON THE SPOT.

If we're in the toy store or grocery store and Barbara has a tantrum, I first try to find an empty aisle and then I reason with her. If that doesn't work, and she's still pounding her hands on the floor, I tell her, "If you don't stop that this instant, I'll have to take you to the car and spank you." I'm careful *never* to spank her in public. If this announcement still does not get results, I leave everything there except my purse, pick her up bodily, and carry her out to the car. There she will either get more talking or the spanking, followed by a hug—her choice.

I try to reason with her more than spank because spanking is not too effective. She seems to become more rigid than before.

20.
IF THE TANTRUM OCCURS
IN A STORE,
RETURN ANYTHING YOU BOUGHT
FOR THE CHILD.

Doreen would most often have temper tantrums in a store, and it was usually because I wouldn't buy her exactly what she wanted. If this occurred, I would return everything I had bought her that day and we would leave. The first time I did this, she kept on crying. The second time, she remembered how disappointed she'd been the last time that the things she'd wanted were returned.

Doreen has not had a third tantrum in a store since trying this method.

AFTERWORD

Take a Deep Breath. . .and Pray

Rejoice always, pray without ceasing, in everything give
thanks; for this is the will of God in Christ Jesus for you.

1 THESSALONIANS 5:16–18

A woman in my Sunday school class shared the following story one week. Since all of us are parents, we empathized with what she'd gone through. Here's how she told it.

From the moment I heard the voice on the other end of the line say, "Mrs. Young? This is Chadwick Elementary School calling," I knew I would not enjoy the next few minutes. I was right.

"I just wanted to let you know," the voice continued, "that your daughter, Laurie, is not in school again today."

"Again today?" I questioned. "What does that mean?"

"Well, I assumed you knew that Laurie was not in school yesterday either. Is she ill?"

"Not yet, but she will be in about two hours when I get home from work."

"I see." The voice was flat. "We'll trust you to take care of it, then?"

"Oh, yes, I shall. Believe me."

I hung up the phone and thought of my twelve-year-old Laurie, wondering what beguiling excuse she'd use this time. My thoughts were still on her when the phone rang again. This time it was my ten-year-old son, Jacob. He was sobbing.

"Mom, I think you'd better come home right away."

"What's happened?" I cried.

"There's been a little accident—"

"How little?" I interrupted.

"Well," he hemmed and hawed, "maybe not so little. I took my bike over to the field for a couple of runs and ran head-on into this other kid."

"Oh, Jacob. Are you all right?"

"Almost, but the bike is totaled and I think I've broken my arm. It really hurts and just dangles. Can you come home and take me to the hospital?"

"Yes, of course. I'll be there in a half hour."

Luckily, since my boss is also a parent, he graciously let me leave work early, knowing, though, that I would still have to punch out and lose two hours' pay. *Why are husbands always out of town when things go wrong?* I thought while fighting the traffic.

When I got home I dashed inside and found Jacob ready to go and my delinquent Laurie in a twitter.

"Mom, Fritzy just threw up all over the couch," she wailed. Fritzy is our German shepherd.

"On the couch?" I groaned. "Why can't he throw up on the floor like any other self-respecting dog? Now it will be oozing in between the cushions and leaving a stain. Laurie, you'll have to clean it up—"

"Me?"

"Yes, you, and when I get home, we're going to have a little talk. Right now I'm taking Jacob to the hospital."

I hurried into the bedroom to get my checkbook and ran smack into Benji, our nine-year-old.

"Mom," he said, grabbing my arm tightly, "have you seen my baseball glove and bat?"

"No, dear, I haven't, and I don't have time to look now. I'm taking Jacob to the hospital."

"Mom," he persisted, "this is important. I have a Little League game in one hour and I have to have my glove and bat."

"Benji," I said, facing him, trying to be calm, "I don't know where your glove is. Use someone else's."

"I can't do that," he explained in a louder tone, staring at me as though I were daft. "I have to have my own. I can't hit with anyone else's bat."

"Sorry, babe, can't help you now."

Out the door I scurried, with Jacob trailing behind, in pain.

By the time I saw my bedroom again, at eight-thirty that night, I had had it. Four hours in the emergency room is not my idea of a fun evening. I sat with my second cup of coffee, reflecting on the broken arm, the dog mess, Laurie's truancy, and Benji's tragic baseball loss. I thought kids were supposed to be a blessing.

I heard the front door open and the voice of our oldest son, sixteen-year-old John, home from his job at McDonald's. He eventually poked his head in the bedroom door. "Hi, Mom. How's it going?"

"Don't ask."

"Had a bad day?"

"Oh, no, just the usual. Nothing out of the ordinary. How was work?"

"Fine."

"No problems? You didn't break a foot or burn the french fries or get in an accident on the way home?"

"Hey, no, Mom."

"That's good," I sighed. *At least one child is okay,* I thought with relief.

"I just hope Dad won't be too upset about the ticket I got."

I sat upright. "Ticket? What ticket? You weren't caught speeding again, were you? You know how your father and I felt about the last one."

"I. . .I guess you could say I was speeding," came the slow response.

"How fast, John?"

"Not bad. Only forty miles per hour."

"In what kind of zone?"

"Twenty-five."

"*You were driving forty in a twenty-five-mile zone?* It's going to cost you an arm and a leg."

"Yeah, plus I didn't have my license. I don't know what happened to my billfold. I hope I didn't lose it at the restaurant."

"Well, don't come to us for the money for that ticket, young man. This is all your party."

"But Mom, I'm broke now. You and Dad can loan me the money for a while, can't you?"

"No, we can't. I only have thirty-seven cents in my purse and I don't get paid for another week." I stood up. "Besides, I'm running away from home."

"Oh, yeah? When are you leaving?"

I stared at this child of my body. Then I laughed out loud—and hugged him. "Before I leave," I said, standing back to gaze into his teasing face, "I'm going to take a deep breath. . .and pray!"

"Good idea, Mom." He gave me a peck on the cheek. "After that, can we talk about a loan?"

1.
RELAX.

We have to remember that all children are raised by amateurs—that's us, the parents—at least the first time around. But our kids are amateurs, too. They don't know any more about being a kid than we do about being a parent. So relax, and goof along together with your kids.

2.
DON'T BE
TOO PROTECTIVE.

Parents make two related mistakes: We are too protective and we don't like to release our children. From the day our babies are born we should start letting them go, little by little, as they are able to handle such freedoms. Let them make some of their own decisions instead of you making every one for them. You don't want your children becoming adults but still depending on you to do everything for them.

It is possible to overprotect a child. Don't put too many restrictions on him. He has to learn some painful lessons for himself. That's not to say you shouldn't be careful and concerned, but a person only learns to run after walking becomes second nature.

Our greatest gift to our children is to release them to explore God's world, always letting them know that He loves them, and that we are always behind them for support, should they need us. Their greatest gift to us is to become mature, capable, and independent individuals who love the Lord with all their being.

3.
START TRAINING YOUNG.

Many of the problems parents have are the result of improper training from day one. By the time a child is five most of his patterns and habits have been established. The person who says, "I'm going to wait until Johnny is in school before I start guiding him," is kidding himself.

4.
EXPECT
GOOD BEHAVIOR.

Kids must learn at an early age that there is behavior that is accepted, and behavior that is not accepted. That's the way the world is.

5.
LISTEN.

Find out what your child is trying to tell you before you lose your temper over bad behavior. "Tell me why you did that so I'll understand," you can say to her. Then listen to her response.

6.
WORK IT OUT
BEFORE YOU FIGHT IT OUT.

"A soft answer turns away wrath, But a harsh word stirs up anger." (Proverbs 15:1).
There will always be rough roads through parenting. Diplomacy

works just as well in the hallways of your household as in the mighty corridors of the United Nations. Listening is far more difficult than spanking. Physical punishment must be last on the list of options.

7.
BE THERE.

We get so busy with our social lives, both inside and outside the church. We're busy taking care of the house. We're busy working. Where do our kids fit in? You'll have thirty or forty years after the kids are grown to do your own thing. While they're with you, do their thing.

8.
PRAISE MORE.
CRITICIZE LESS.

Some parents are disciplinarians, and some disciplinarians like to criticize. It's easy to criticize but far better to praise. Kids need praise to grow emotionally stable. The compromise? Discipline your children with praise.

9.
TEACH THEM WHO
IS THE PARENT.

While you're teaching your children to be independent, to think and act for themselves, teach them who the parents are. Someone has to be in charge of the household, and it shouldn't be the kids.

10.
WHATEVER YOU THREATEN,
DO IT.

If you say to your child, "You can't go to Jackie's party unless you clean your room," be prepared to carry out that threat. Don't threaten something unrealistic that you either won't do or don't want to do. At the same time don't be afraid to admit when you've been unreasonable. The key is, think before you threaten, and then make the threats stick.

11.
MAKE THE PUNISHMENT
FIT THE CRIME.

A totally unrelated disciplinary action doesn't make the same impression as one that has something to do with what was done wrong. Example: If Caleb spreads grape jelly on the wall, Caleb should clean the grape jelly off the wall. That will discourage him from doing it again more than sending him to his room for an hour.

12.
BELIEVE IN HIM.

If at all possible, believe in your child and let him know you trust him totally. Unless you have proof to the contrary, don't be quick to believe what someone else says about him, especially if he tells another story. Not trusting a truthful child will surely turn him against you. Even if it turns out he's lying to you, the lie is on his conscience. Someday he'll remember that you trusted him.

13.
YOUR DISAPPROVAL SHOULD BE THEIR GREATEST PUNISHMENT.

When there is a loving, trusting relationship between parent and child, your disapproval can be more punishment than restrictions, privileges revoked, or spanking. Let the raising of your voice or frown of disappointment speak to your child's heart. The goal is to bring a child to the place where he respects and loves you enough so that even when tempted to do wrong, he won't give in because he doesn't want your disapproval.

The ultimate goal, of course, is to raise children to feel this way about God—to want never to disappoint Him.

14.
DON'T LEAVE YOUR HUSBAND OR WIFE OUT OF THE FAMILY.

If you don't tell your spouse about your child's bad behavior, the day will surely come when the truth is revealed. Most likely the spouse will be furious with you because he feels like an outsider in his own home. He'll accuse you of not trusting him enough to confide what's been going on. There may be bitterness and the marriage may even flounder.

Trust your spouse and raise your children together.

15.
CHILDREN WANT TO KNOW
WHERE THEY STAND.

They really do want to know how you feel about things. It gives them security if you are stable in your principles. Be honest. In turn, they want you to know what they believe, too. Be able to take it.

16.
MAKE IT ROUTINE.

The best results come when good behavior is part of the routine and treated as an expected occurrence. That means parents must behave routinely as well.

17.
IT TAKES
BOTH PARENTS.

If you're a father, don't leave the responsibility for raising the children to the wife. Don't be too busy. Be there. Stay home. Spend time with your children. They'll eat it up, and grow secure in your love and attention.

18.
TRY A GAB SESSION.

If there are problems within your family, give each person the chance to air his gripes. A gab session is not an easy thing to sit through, but the time should bring you closer together.

And don't wait for a major crisis, when the air is charged with heavy feelings. Have your talks when everyone is in a good mood and can communicate without getting angry, if possible. Get out some popcorn and apples and say, "Here are some things that have been bothering me."

Most of all, pray together as a family over your problems.

19.
DON'T BE AFRAID
TO "GROUND" YOUR CHILD,
OR PUT HER ON RESTRICTION.

It doesn't hurt kids to be grounded, and sometimes it becomes a badge of greatness. If parents are too nice or too easy or too good, a kid may be made fun of by his friends. Listen carefully and someday you may hear your child say with a swagger, "Naw, I can't. I'm grounded!"

20.
DON'T USE FEAR
AS A PARENTING TOOL.

Sometimes I hear a parent say, "If you don't behave yourself, I'll turn out all the lights. . .lock you in the closet. . .leave you behind" and so on. When we have long forgotten the incident, children will remember and may develop terrible fears based on our threats.

21.
I Want Him to Be
What He Wants to Be.

Don't pressure a child to fulfill your dreams. Let him be himself. Support his ambitions if at all possible.

22.
Learn Your Child's
Behavior Cycles,
and Be prepared.

Some children have behavior cycles. They may be fine for a few weeks—cooperative, behaving themselves, and pleasant to be around. Then they may start to be naughty, obnoxious, or even unbearable. Knowing these moods are coming will help you deal with them, and keep yourself from reaching the breaking point.

23.
Stimulate
That Little Mind.

"Oh, she's just a kid, what does she know?" Have you ever heard someone say that? We know that during her first five years a child learns more than at any other time in her life. Stimulate that mind and spirit. Show her the world of imagination and truth and faith. Help her soar. Notice I said "help," not "push," as in perform. Her passionate interest may not be uncovered unless you expose her to the "riches" of life.

24.
GOD IS
ALWAYS THERE.

"Trust in the LORD with all your heart, And lean not on your own understanding; In all your ways acknowledge Him, And He shall direct your paths." (Proverbs 3:5–6).